Happy Christmas.

Much love.

Aunt Margaret

Dec. 1988

FISHING FROM MY ANGLE

FISHING
FROM
MY ANGLE

Tales by
CYRIL HOLBROOK

DAVID & CHARLES
Newton Abbot London North Pomfret (Vt)

Line illustrations by Ged Melling

British Library Cataloguing in Publication Data

Holbrook, Cyril
  Fishing from my angle.
  1. Fishing – Great Britain
  I. Title
  799.1'092'4   SH605
  ISBN 0–7153–9124–0

Photoset in Linotron Sabon
by Northern Phototypesetting Co, Bolton
and printed in Great Britain
by Billings Limited, Worcester
for David & Charles Publishers plc
Brunel House Newton Abbot Devon

Published in the United States of America
by David & Charles Inc
North Pomfret Vermont 05053 USA

Preface

CYRIL HOLBROOK admits to being lucky in that, as an angler, he has been involved with fish and fishing tackle most of his working life as a journalist.

Born in the Fens, his boyhood fishing background drew him into editing the angling pages of the *Eastern Evening News* in Norwich for eight years while the Broads were at their peak. The chance to beach and boat fish was too good to miss when his family lived in Cromer for four years and, shortly after moving to Peterborough, he was actually asked to join *Angling Times*.

After four years on the world's Number One angling publication, he edited *Tackle & Guns*, the trade title, for ten years. While working closely with the industry that provides anglers with their gear, he had the chance to try out all the latest equipment as carbon, boron and Kevlar came on to the scene. As he says, 'For an average angler, that has got to be pretty lucky.'

Having written literally millions of words on the sport and the trade, he looks – in this first book – at why people fish, how they fish and many of the characters who have helped add to the pleasure he has derived from his fishing. He also sounds a warning for the future that affects not only those who fish, and dares to suggest the scrapping of the rod licence.

It is a book which will bring a smile to anyone who has ever held a fishing rod and give them something to think about . . . as well as giving those who don't fish an understanding of those who do.

Contents

The Fishing Day

HAVE you looked out over fields of dew before the night is
done,
And felt earth's heartbeat quicken with the coming of the sun?
Then cast your line and waited for that sudden, searing run
That makes cold hours forgotten as your pulse begins to drum.

Have you wondered at the unseen power that's surging in the
depths,
And caught a glimpse of silver scales that makes you hold your
breath?
Then, with arm aching, prayed a bit as it comes towards the
net
Before that trembling moment that you know you'll not
forget.

Have you shared the feeling Caesar felt with thumbs up long
ago;
Returned to Nature what She gave and let the vanquished go?
Then, wet from splash of paddle tail, still basking in the glow
You wonder if you'll be believed – and will the monster grow?

Have you seen the owl start flying as the bats come out to play
And known that happy sorrow as the gold turns into grey?
Then headed home to face the world, refreshed in such a way
That no one but the angler knows who's had a fish-filled day.

Dedication

THE majority of authors can dedicate a book to virtually anyone they like. Anglers, however, have no such prerogative being honour bound to offer their work as a humble tribute to their wives.

The 'golfing widow' is the recipient of wide sympathy, but it is surely the 'angling widow' who is deserving of most condolence. After all, does the golf ball smell like a pint of pinkies? Does the bag of clubs ever become as mud encrusted as the rod holdall? Does the golfer feel called upon to steal from the sewing basket after turning it upside down in search of a thread to match the colour of a hatching insect? And is nail varnish 'borrowed' to secure the whipping on clubs as it is on rods?

Without doubt, those married to anglers can claim to have a rougher time of it.

So this dedication is paid to all angling widows everywhere – especially to Anne, my very own member of that world-wide sisterhood.

Introduction

IF only we could all go fishing twenty-four hours earlier, arriving at the water for each trip the day before we actually get there, how many more fish we would catch, and how much bigger they would be.

This conclusion comes from the number of times Britain's 4 million anglers are told 'You should have been here yesterday' whenever and wherever we go. It is certain, too, that in a French, Italian, German, Spanish – and even in a Trans-Atlantic – accent, fishermen all over the world are told the same thing.

'I've got one!' is probably the first shout to come in a piping voice from the excited throat of the youngster taking that first step on the road to becoming one of the most fortunate of men – an angler.

It isn't long though before he hears those other words that will haunt him as long as he fishes. There will always be someone who will say, 'You ought to have seen what came out yesterday, they were taking everything anybody threw at them.'

Or – 'The way the cod came in on last night's tide, there must have been twenty rods bent at once along the beach no end of times.'

Or – and this is the worst of all – 'Everybody had a netful before the weather changed yesterday afternoon.'

Every angler knows the sort of thing.

It isn't always the person who did the catching from whom you hear the news direct. In fact, it's normally a third party and frequently one not totally unconnected with the source you are buying your bait from . . . and from whom you go on to buy the new tackle you'll need if you are to emulate the feats he's telling you about.

It's all done with the best of intentions, however, the prime object genuinely being to help us catch more fish. You only have to consider the number of books and magazines on the subject to realise just how anglers love to tell each other about what they have caught. And the vast majority of this information is aimed at giving others pointers to ways in which they can increase their enjoyment.

Most anglers, however, don't want to complicate their sport with a lot of technicalities. True, they would be delighted to win a big open match, or tame a shark, or net a double-figure rainbow, should lightning strike. The expense, the time and – above all – the dedication involved to make these things happen without a great deal of luck being required, are not for them. They fish for the fun of it. The rod is often an excuse to sit somewhere they simply enjoy being, whether it's a swim they know well or a charter boat they feel comfortable aboard.

If a few fish happen along, well, that'll be fine. If they don't, it isn't going to ruin anybody's day. (Well, not completely anyway.)

This army of casual fishermen is usually covered by that glorious name 'pleasure anglers'. Perhaps it would be more honest to describe them by a label I have sometimes applied to myself: 'lazy anglers'.

We tend not to spend too much time in travelling to distant, possibly more productive venues but to fish locally. We derive huge satisfaction from establishing a link with nature in which telephones and twentieth-century pressures play no part.

Good fortune has meant that taking the easiest fishing on offer has led me to prolific coarse waters, let me learn to cast a fly for trout, and acquainted me with men whose lives are atuned to the sea.

Though winning the odd open and lots of trophies in local matches, I always turned down the chance to fish in Nationals because of a desire not to be 'herded' in the way that's necessary if a thousand men and their gear are to arrive at their designated swims on time. It's just not for me. Like the bulk of Izaak Walton's successors, competing with other anglers could spoil the fun of taking on the fish for me. Most of us don't have a very impressive big fish list either; personally it's because I've never been able to ignore the chance of a nice net of roach or dace in favour of the rod hours that have to be put in to turn up the monsters.

So here are tales of where the enjoyment has come from – the fish, the places and, above all, the people whose love of fishing in all its forms it has been my good fortune to share. Of course, they may help someone catch more fish. After all, nobody tells another angler about fishing without passing on something useful. My real hope, however, is that they will lead to some of my fellow pleasure anglers deriving more of it from their outings . . . as much as they would have had yesterday!

1

Preconceptions

THAT helpful advice that incorporates the 'You should have been here yesterday' part, always includes one flaw . . . it encourages preconceived ideas.

Like all the written reports about what has been taken recently and the baits, flies and methods that guarantee success, it fills the angler full of hope and is inclined to put him in a kind of mental straitjacket. When you learn that several people have taken the type of fish you are after in a certain way, it is difficult to start fishing using purely your own skill and judgement.

This local knowledge can be vital when all is said and done and these people have actually caught the fish. What they did worked so you have a pattern to follow. Wouldn't it be foolish not to follow their lead?

The trouble is, it's all too easy to find you've stopped thinking and looking for yourself, and you're simply following the well-worn path. The most successful fishermen are those who find today's answers more quickly than anybody else. They listen to all the available information about yesterday – indeed, there is a virtual spy network out there collating it all for those who take the time to tap into it. But they don't accept these reports blindly. They apply their own logic to the situation, not necessarily inventing something new all the time but making use of some ploy that worked before somewhere, or one they heard of that worked for someone else.

The key is confidence; a belief that the plan you formulate for today is going to work, even if it's not the same as the one that worked yesterday.

Everybody hits one of those patches when they simply know they're not going to catch anything whatever they do. And that's not the time to try your brilliant and original scheme. How many really good ideas have been written off and never heard of because they were conceived in desperation in one of those periods during which nothing was going to be caught whatever the angler did, perhaps simply because there were no fish there?

It's obvious really that something different is only worth giving a go when you are sure there are feeding fish out there. We all do the opposite though; we stick to proven baits or fly patterns when we have feeding fish in front of us and, more often than not, the new idea isn't brought into play until the tried and tested fish-takers have failed.

It's a bit like the situation that happens regularly in cricket . . . the guy who doesn't normally bowl only gets a chance when the batsmen are dug in and knocking all the recognised bowlers all over the county. It's not really a fair test, is it?

One of the wonderful things about fishing – as well as its most infuriating facet – is that there are always circumstances you can't control, even factors that affect the fish that we aren't fully aware of.

However you master the best equipment; whatever experiments you undertake; no matter what lengths you go to to make sure your bait is the best being offered; the final say is with a wild creature that has to open its mouth and take your hook inside.

Overnight rain, a drop in temperature or a shift in the wind are all among the more obvious things that can spell doom for your best laid plans, or – on other days – make them work.

Why, for instance, should a lowering of air pressure affect creatures living in another element? The best guess I've heard is that it is something to do with the dissolved oxygen content of the water but, whatever the truth, there is no doubt that the best chance of success is when the barometer's needle is going up, not backwards.

In fact, there are waters which are virtually a barometer themselves. The Welland is one such river where fish react to changes in the weather before we even know they're coming.

Which is why you see matchmen tottering down the bank

under such a load of equipment and bait. Having to pick a peg number from a hat means he has no idea where he may have to sit, so he doesn't know what he needs. The upshot is he has to take as much as he can – just in case.

The trout angler may feel less weighed down, but many travel to the water with several rods and a multiplicity of lines, to say nothing of that huge collection of flies and lures, the vast majority of which are never likely to get near the water.

Of course there are occasions when preconceived notions and planning play a larger part. The specimen hunter knows most about them. Having found a water that holds worthy examples of the species he is after, the tendency is to do as much pre-baiting as possible – to get the fish used to eating what he is going to put on his hook and educate them to feed where he can reach them.

The start of the season is the time when this procedure is at its peak. The close season has made past failures fade in the mind, confidence is restored and, because the angler cannot fish, he has time to prepare for the first outing of a new year.

The range of ingredients used in 'secret' recipes is phenomenal – from Fiente (which is dried and milled pigeon droppings, and French pigeons at that), through every human food flavouring and colouring, to Norwegian tar.

Others go for natural baits. One angler spent a month increasing the frequency with which he introduced cockles into a water near his home. He had heard of their success on another heavily fished water and, as this was a similar spot and held good tench and bream, the idea was to get them feeding on his bait by mid-June. Pints and pints went in on that eve-of-season finale to the bait bombardment.

Next morning, he sat without a bite as tench and bream were caught by those around him, people who had simply rolled up and used bread and maggots like they always had. The fish weren't the monsters he had planned for. But they were fish.

Undaunted, he stuck it out fishless for a fortnight during which he witnessed several good catches by other people. Then he gave up cockles for good.

Another opening day which showed the danger of the blinkered approach was shared with two other anglers on a Norfolk lake. 'Full of tench' it was, and we cleared swims and baited accordingly.

One of us had three tench, granted, while we other pair contented ourselves with little roach and bream. Then a big, black back humped alongside my float. The dorsal fin was too far back for it to be anything but a pike.

Borrowing a heavy leger rod, I soon had a pike of just over 10lb on the bank. Just in case, a second cast was made. Ten-pound pike number two was soon caught, followed by a third that was a bit bigger. A 'Jack' of around 4lb rounded off the morning.

They weren't what I had gone for, but they gave us some fun we hadn't bargained for. All because that one glimpse of a surfacing pike woke me from my dream of tench.

Keeping an open mind is seldom easy.

2

Uncle Charlie

EVERY boy should have an Uncle Charlie. Indeed, I suspect that every angler did have one whether it was a 'real' uncle or just the mentor who opened the doors of his mind to show the paths of pleasure along which a fishing rod could lead him.

Mine was my mother's brother whose calloused carpenter's hands could tie dainty knots. He always wore a cap, probably accounting for his premature baldness, and behind his glasses were twinkling eyes which missed very little.

I had been fishing with my father before uncle's influence affected me. In fact, the transport for the first day's fishing I remember was a seat on the crossbar of Dad's bike. I can still recall the frustration of being kept away from the steep bank where all the interesting things were going on.

It is always frightening, the way in which children ape the actions of their elders for good or ill. It's as well fishing is one of the good things in life, for from that day onwards, I couldn't wait to go fishing – like the men.

A man called Hitler focussed people's minds on less enjoyable things for a while, but by the time summer Saturday afternoons were for fishing again, I was old enough to tag along. Dad, Uncle Charlie and a regular assortment of their workmates used to cycle the four miles to their favourite bank with me and other lads in tow.

Personal experience has taught me that boys are inclined to take more notice of advice from others than from their own fathers. Certainly uncle was the counsellor and guide for me.

My father was the most relaxed angler of all time. He would set up a rod that had cost him 17s 6d before the war when he was earning not much more than that a week, dump in some groundbait, tip his trilby over his eyes to keep the sun out and

wait to see what came along. Contemplative communion with nature at its best.

Uncle Charlie was different. He really hunted the fish, for ever trying something new; working at it and trying to tempt anything in the swim to bite. He never match fished, perhaps because deep down he knew what I came to realise years later – that he wasn't as good a fisherman as he made everybody else, as well as himself, believe.

Confidence was never a problem and he was utterly convinced of the wisdom and rightness of his own decisions. His competitive edge made him determined to have more fish than the rest of us in the miniscule keepnets we used then. But he always had time to teach me and the other youngsters what to do.

'That's it,' he would say, 'just move that bottom shot down a bit nearer the hook then keep moving the quill up until it's cocking to one side. Then you'll know your bait's on the bottom and when a bream picks it up you'll see just what he's doing.'

'Wait! Wait! Don't hurry him! Give him time!' he would urge when youthful impatience made us want to strike at every movement. Nerves a-tingle, we would hold our breath as the float dithered and lay flat. 'Wait till it slides under,' he would warn, making us slow down to the pace of the bream finding his food in the Fenland mud.

Surprisingly, we never felt he interfered though he obviously did regularly. Perhaps the bond was strong because he had had two daughters both of whom had died by the time they were five. It was only growing older that I realised that it was not all a one-way trade and that I wasn't the only one to reap a reward from those fishing outings.

By today's standards the tackle was primitive and most lads wouldn't go at all now unless they had something much better. My rod was whole bamboo but for the top 2 feet which were of split cane. All the rest, including the wooden centre-pin reel, groundbait, sixpennyworth of maggots and the sandwiches, went into an ex-Fire Service gas mask bag until I graduated to a creel made from a bicycle basket.

We caught fish though. Perch and roach were pleased to oblige, gudgeon and the hated cocky ruffe and eels were usually present, and somebody normally caught a bream or two, mostly small and silver but occasionally big and bronze. And there were pike.

No one in the Fens knew there was such a thing as a pike rod then. Later a cousin and I bought converted tank aerials that did the job, and mine – reringed, rehandled and repainted many times – always seemed to be the rod to turn up a pike anywhere.

In pre-tank aerial days, the format was to take a neatly shaped piece of kindling, wrap bike dress guard round it, pop a barrel bung up the end and tie on a snap-tackle. If a pike 'struck' along the river, you put a livebait on the only bona fide piece of the equipment, threw it out, pegged it down – and left it.

We were fortunate in that the local bailiff had an artificial leg. As we always went well along the bank, we could spot him coming with his 'swinger' miles away.

'Peg Leg's coming!' someone would call and there would be a hasty scrambling in the rushes. Lines were pulled in and hidden and the bait put back in the keepnet. Once the 'tickets' had been checked and he had gone, the rig was brought back into use.

We caught a lot of pike in that largely unsporting way. They all went into somebody's pantry, too. Don't forget rationing made them valuable and we (well, certainly the youngsters) knew no better.

That 'cull' did no harm to what was to become a famous pike water later on. The water authority even introduced their own pike and zander removal scheme years later.

It wasn't as though we were surreptitious either. The approved method of carrying larger pike home was to have them trailing from the bike handlebars.

The luxury of motorised transport came when Eric, who worked with uncle, bought himself an ancient red Austin Seven van. It wouldn't go much faster than we could bike without real risk of explosion and only he and uncle could sit

in the front. But it did mean that all the tackle could be carried – including folding chairs now – with me and cousin David in the back as well to stop it rattling about.

We even went further afield and one new water was a lake that had been formed when gravel was scraped up into a railway embankment. It was very shallow and with our gear we couldn't cast into more than a couple of feet of water. Catch one or two, then wait until they got over the fright and moved back on to the bait; that was the pattern. Trouble was, sometimes they didn't come back.

So Norman brought along his blow-up rubber dinghy. 'I can get out to the deeper water and catch a lot more fish,' he reasoned. He was right, of course, and soon he and Eric were taking it in turns in the boat. Which was fine until Eric went after a pike he had seen feeding well out. Once hooked, it turned out to be around 10lb and the pike and Eric were soon going round and round together in fine style.

Of course, no one had a landing net big enough then, and it was when Eric went to gaff it that the trouble began. You've guessed it; he missed and stuck the point in the boat.

Playing the fish, baling out the hissing dinghy and paddling needed one more hand than Eric had available. Give credit where it's due though, that pike was landed and without any help save futile instructions from the hysterical gallery.

Alan's entry into the drink was even more spectacular. He was a boy who lived next door to my uncle. One spot we went to meant crossing a drain by an old brick bridge to get to the main river. The parapets had been washed away in the floods of successive winters that have since completed the job of destroying the bridge completely.

Cattle summer-pastured on the lush grass and a gate barred their exit and our way across. The procedure was to heft your bike on to your shoulder, swing round the post over the gap where the parapet should have been and on to the bridge the other side.

'Can you manage all right?' 'Pass me your box.' 'Shall I give you a hand?' We were all going through the routine when there was a shriek. Alan's hand had slipped in mid-swing and he plunged 7 or 8 feet into the water, bike and all. He clambered out covered in weed and mud unhurt, only to be sent back for his bike. 'Well, there's no sense everybody getting soaked,' uncle pointed out.

All Alan could keep muttering was 'What'll mum say?' Which was also the thought exercising Uncle Charlie's mind. So Alan spent the rest of the day wrapped in a blanket in a farmer's kitchen with his clothes draped around the cooking range so that he was presentable enough by the time we went home for his future outings – and Uncle Charlie's hide – to be salvaged.

The renovation of that farmhouse led to some fine fishing for me and a pal. Rumour had it that it had been built by Charles II when the Fens were drained. Certainly when they stripped the parlour I was there to count thirty-two layers of wallpaper so it had clearly been there a while. Every day during that summer holiday, the lorry took the men out of the yard at half past seven. With them were Michael and me with our bikes and fishing gear.

While they set to work, we rode down the bank into what has since become a bird sanctuary where we would probably not see a soul all day.

What we did come across on one occasion was a couple of visiting anglers using tackle which let them cast so far we couldn't believe it. They had the new fixed-spool reels and though it seems we've never fished without them, it's incredible just how relatively recent the change was.

Another milestone was Uncle Charlie's return from holiday, with some new line. Nylon it was called and horribly springy thick stuff it was by modern lights. But although it spiralled from his centre-pin in ugly coils, it did float without having to be drawn through a tallow candle like all our old cotton lines had to be.

Everyone wanted to see this wonder and be shown the special knots he had discovered to join it to the yard of bottom gut. He was really King of the River for a while that summer.

As well as fishing, we learned a lot of country lore from the Fenmen we fished with. Of course we were taught 'When the

wind is in the east . . .', 'Red sky at night . . .', and well known weather pointers. And did you know that if all the cows in a herd turn their backs to the wind it's going to rain?

Not all of it was so reliable. One of them, for instance, insisted that it was putting the clocks back that caused the weather to break up every autumn.

'I wish they'd leave 'em alone,' he would say. 'As soon as they muck the clocks about that weather'll turn cold and rainy.'

He was also the man who looked at a council gang clearing the pavements one snowy January and commented seriously, 'The rate they're working it'll take all summer to shift this lot!'

3
The Norfolk Connection

ANGLERS themselves know that the generally held belief that they don't always stick strictly to the facts is totally untrue. But there is no doubt that a certain amount of embroidery which could more accurately be described as 'kidology' plays a large part in the sport.

A fair way of summing it up would be 'Telling the truth, nothing but the truth but not quite the whole truth.' Even some angling writers have been masters at letting everybody into 95 per cent of their secrets while holding on to the last vital piece of the jigsaw.

Anyone can be sent to the right water but with the wrong bait or the wrong way of presenting it, but it is in match fishing that the art of confusing other fishermen is at its zenith. From hurling great balls of groundbait to the far bank then fishing quietly down the side, to letting little fish splash a lot on the surface to make others think you're doing better than you really are, it goes on all the time.

A classic example of how to ensure that at least some of the opposition waste valuable time was told me by that great Norfolk fisherman Ken Smith who won the National – then the All England – in 1960.

Ken had a mischievous sense of humour and, when a set of weighted floats he made proved just too heavy – sinking gently all on their own – he decided not to let the experiment be totally unproductive.

At the next open match on the River Bure he casually dropped them 'accidentally' at the draw, knowing that with his reputation they were as likely to be returned as samples left lying around in a bank.

'I don't know what happened to the others,' he said, 'but

one fellow who picked one of them up and slipped it into his pocket was pegged near me. The floats looked perfect and he fell for it, obviously thinking that if I'd made them specially for the match, he'd use one too.

'I kept an eye on him as he gradually took off shot after shot and moved them about for half an hour before he realised what was happening. That was one angler I didn't have to worry about.'

When he won that Broadland National, swingtips and quivertips were in their infancy and it was one of his innovations that *did* work that he used to change his life. And that win really did alter his future, for with the proceeds from that victory he gave up his job in a Norwich shoe factory and opened his own tackle shop in the city.

His bite indicator was several strands of really thick nylon, at least 80lb, glued and whipped together. When fixed to a rod top, it didn't hang like a swingtip or curve smoothly like a quiver. It bent a section at a time when bites came as first the single, then the double, then each additional thickness bent, giving a very positive indication. It's surprising that no one has ever produced one like it commercially.

Ken became a friend when he started to write for the Norwich *Eastern Evening News* every week. It's strange how little things as well as winning Nationals can affect your life, and I was editing the angling pages because of a chance remark which was a quote from a little book my father had had.

'Bream fishing begins with a wheelbarrow' the forgotten author had written. It's a nice phrase and not bad when you consider the amount of groundbait you need to introduce on a big water with hefty shoals.

When it was dropped into a conversation not long after I joined the paper, a couple of heads nodded and the 'new boy' who had revealed himself as an angler was assigned to sorting out the fishing pages every Tuesday afternoon.

Another of our regular contributors was Peter Collins who wrote under the pen-name 'Broadland Otter'. Several years later we worked together on *Angling Times* after I caught up with him again in Peterborough. Respected throughout angling, he made his mark on the national weekly before becoming editor of *Sea Angler* magazine. More than once, I reminded him of the time when 'Broadland Otter' wrote off sea fishing as 'all chuck it and chance it' and said he would never get involved with it.

The first time I fished with Peter was when he did a pike feature for the *Times* on a lake in North Norfolk. It was a bitter, frosty morning and it didn't warm up a lot all day. Everything looked against the assembled party but, though nothing big turned up, we took twenty-eight pike.

Though we had gone to great lengths to make sure we had plenty of livebaits, they all fell to deadbaits, most of them from a patch I had covered with mashed sprats when we got there. It's a dodge I've used to groundbait for pike many times and, if fish are around, it does seem to make them hungry.

It was on the way home that day that I literally put my foot in it in a way you wouldn't expect a Fenman to do. Cattle had been churning up the gateway until it was calf-deep in mud (sorry about the pun). With rods, gear, bait buckets and nets I was well weighted above the centre of gravity and, when suction held a wellington solid in the goo, I was faced with a swift choice between plodding bootless to the gate or falling over in it.

I strode on barefoot. That's what you get for having boots big enough to get two thick pairs of socks in.

My Norfolk connection had begun much earlier, for my father's family came from the county and one of his three brothers still lived there. If it was Uncle Charlie who taught me the basics – including a lot of bad habits along the way – it was Uncle Ken from Norwich who made me aware of the wider world going on outside our Fenland town.

Uncles Sid and Les both came on holiday from Birmingham and fished with us. Sid, who was always full of fun, thoroughly enjoyed it, the open Fens being about as big a contrast as you could find from Longbridge. By the time I was 11, though, I was teaching him.

Les was much more taciturn. His pride was a long green-heart rod so heavy a mere boy like me couldn't fish with it. He always fished in his stockinged feet 'for comfort' and ended the day in the nearest pub, sometimes doing a bit of prospecting at lunchtime, too.

Anyway, they usually had their families along, with Mum bringing along a picnic spread for everybody. And every boy knows you can't fish seriously when there are women around!

Uncle Ken was different, bringing stories of fish he caught on the Broads and tales of wonderful, far-off rivers like the Yare and the Thurne. Now and again my aunt would trap him. 'You old fossil,' she would say, 'you're not sneaking off again today. You're taking me out.' Most of the time he would escape, though, and spend the day with his rod on one of the Fenland rivers.

One or other of his brothers would always tell the tale of how Ken had got up early to poach trout from the Glaven while staying with their Uncle Tom. And he was the gamekeeper! Ken would just roar with laughter and nobody doubted it. Auntie Elsie didn't stand a chance.

He was also more thorough in his preparation than anyone I had come across before. Rationed bread would appear for bait along with chicken meal from the local mill. Mother would find herself cooking potatoes to feed the fish.

'Look at that,' he'd say, producing a bag of fluffy groundbait or a pile of cricket-ball sized, neatly moulded fish inducers.

He used bigger hooks than the locals and covered them with big lumps pinched from a loaf of bread a lot, too.

'Why, I caught a bream weighing 2½lb from the Yare with a piece of flake twice as big as that only a fortnight ago!'

With anglers from the town now popping up to the Trent for an outing and several going to Ireland to fish every year, it's difficult to realise just how insular we were. Every week we read of people going as far as the south of France to catch carp or piking in the Scottish lochs. Forty years back, a boat on the Ouse twelve miles away was an adventure and we even did that with Uncle Ken.

But it was his Norfolk link that made me feel I knew something about the area by the time I joined the *Evening*

News. One of my better ideas was that I should become the novice and fish with the master – Ken Smith. 'I'll write features on the difference between the class angler and his pupil,' I explained. 'Everyone will be able to learn from my experiences.' The editor said he didn't like it.

Realisation as to why came shortly afterwards when he moved to take over our sister morning paper. Their angling coverage was pepped up straight away by an angling 'beginner' on their features staff being put under the wing of none other than Ken Smith.

He was a Yorkshire lad called Colin Dyson who subsequently returned to Sheffield where he has written and edited several angling books as well as becoming editor of *Coarse Angler* magazine.

During our time in Norfolk we often fished together in boat matches on the Broads. Most pairs fished against each other as well as those in the other boats but we reasoned that pulling fish to two lots of groundbait close together split a shoal, unsettled them and gave us less time to catch them. So we shared one swim. We've sat with our floats within a yard of each other all day and caught fish for fish more than once.

Since we both moved on, our paths have crossed at intervals and we've never been able to resist harking back to the days when Ken influenced us both. A fish we often refer to is the 21½lb pike Colin caught on Hickling Broad. I knew there was a fish in a corner of the rush beds by the way the livebait swam away every time it was put anywhere near. But I was using a centre-pin reel and couldn't quite make it into the table-top sized patch behind the marginal fringe.

Colin had a fixed spool on his rod. 'Go on, you have a go,' I said. First cast, his float disappeared straight into the reeds. Fortune smiled, however, and the fish moved right back out again. Colin led it gently clear of obstruction and then struck. After a hectic scrap it was a treat to see the beautiful fish safely in the boat, even if I hadn't caught it and it was one of my big single hooks he was using to prevent snagging in the reeds.

Of course, any mention of the Broads and pike has to include the name of the man whose fame spread far beyond Norfolk – Dennis Pye.

Stories of how many 20lb-plus fish he caught abounded and though he wrote his own book about catching them, his success generally came from keeping things simple and spending an immense amount of time on waters that held big fish.

No doubt some of his big pike were recorded several times as he caught them again to make the numbers up. When he wasn't in his fish and chip shop he was in his boat with his Alsatian on the upper Thurne waters which were in terrific form.

His knowledge of those vast waters is illustrated by the lovely story of the man for whom he made a dream come true. They met in a country inn where the visitor said he had wanted to catch a 20-pounder for years but had never made it. Dennis promised to make sure he got one.

He took the angler across the broad in his boat and told him, 'Cast your bait a foot off that lily pad', pointing to the exact spot alongside the extensive weedbed. His guest did as he was told. If memory serves me right, the fish he took weighed 22lb when it was boated and witnessed.

Dennis knew where the pike lay all right.

One problem he caused me was his domination of the Silver Fish Contest I ran for the paper. The idea was that the chance of winning the coveted award would inspire anglers who caught good fish in the area to tell us about them. The trouble was that his big fish put the others off, so we changed the format. Instead of comparing the different species of fish by taking them as a percentage of the national record we judged them against the best we had had since the competition started several years before. A pike would virtually have had to beat the record to win the trophy again.

But Dennis beat us at our own game. When he read the new rules, he went out and caught a massive tench which led the way all season – and won it again.

He never did make the British record though. That distinction fell to Peter Hancock whose 40-pounder came shortly before the fish-kill wiped out that unique area. And the fact that that has been bettered from the same system again recently is great news. It's good to hear of records being broken in Norfolk again.

4

Vive la Difference

THOSE unfortunate people who have missed out on the delights of the Gentle Art and don't fish have the greatest difficulty in understanding those of us who do. To many we are mildly eccentric worm-drowners, their attitude being epitomised by the ladies who ask, 'Do you really warm maggots under your tongue in the winter?'

Others take their ignorance to extremes. They categorise us along with those who would like to reintroduce cock-fighting (they use game bird feathers in their flies, don't they?), or those who pump up geese for foie gras. They join the Animal Liberation Front and go round glueing up the doors of tackle shops to prove their dedication to the cause and their own lack of imagination at the same time.

It is difficult to explain to any of the non-angling populace just what it's all about. How can you explain to someone preoccupied with the possibility that worms feel pain the delight of watching a dragonfly emerge and take to the air on a misty morning or the thrill of feeling the tide surge under the keel as you fight an unseen force below.

The only real answer is to take them and let them see for themselves, though the chairperson of your local branch of the League Against Cruel Sports probably wouldn't be the best one to start with. 'Cast not your pearls before swine.'

Better to work your way into it gradually by taking a boy recommended by the vicar or even a couple of stalwarts from the WI choir (they never would come one at a time) before you find yourself having taken on more than you can handle.

This informing of the benighted, however, is still relatively easy when compared with the almost impossible task of overcoming the impregnable and even more stubbornly defended barriers which have been erected between the different facets of the sport of angling over the years.

Broadly speaking, there are three sorts of fishermen: coarse, sea and game.

The coarse anglers are then sub-divided into matchmen, specimen hunters and 'pleasure' anglers.

Sea anglers are lumped into two classes – beach or boat men, which is relatively simple to understand.

Game anglers, however, are a very complicated lot. They come under the main headings of trout, salmon and sea-trout fishermen though fly fishing, spinning and worming branches of all three make it hard to pin them down, some people drifting willy-nilly from section to section at different times of the year and in various parts of the country.

In days gone by it was relatively easy to put an angler in his rightful pigeon-hole and know that he would stay there. Dress was a big help in this. Sea anglers wore oilskins and thigh waders; fly fishermen were attired in plus-fours and funny hats; and coarse anglers dressed up in anything warm left over from the army that kept the rain out of the tops of their wellies.

In more recent times, however, there has been a lot of movement across the various dividing lines. Why, I was even at a meeting not long since at which representatives of all the associations covering all these diverse fishing creeds not only sat down together without anyone coming to blows, but actually came away with some sort of agreement about future co-operation.

When I started fishing that would not only have been impossible, it would have been unthinkable. Then, the matchman knew that anybody who had a fly rod was a toffee-nosed Tory who only went fishing to underline the fact that he could have two miles of river all to himself and kill all the fish he caught if he liked.

Salmon anglers were known by all the others to be just the sort the French got rid of on the guillotine. 'Just watch how we'll set all the bailiffs and ghillies free when our revolution comes' was the attitude.

As for matchmen, they lived in terraced houses that stank

because of the dead things they kept inside to breed maggots on; they worked in factories or down t'pit; and they only stopped swilling beer for five hours on a Sunday . . . mostly!

There were few specialist big fish hunters around. Those who were, were regarded as a bit suspect and not quite being able to make their minds up whether they were proper coarse or game fishermen. They were also generally looked down on by matchmen as being too chicken to 'Put their money where their mouth is' or 'Come out into the open and show what they can do if they're that bloody clever.'

Sea anglers, of course, were primarily concerned with seeing how far they could sling a great lump of lead. They also liked cutting up anything they caught and using such stiff rods aboard boats that nothing had a chance to bend them. Not sporting at all.

No, everybody knew his place in the piscatorial pecking order and believed such foul things of anyone who didn't fish like he did that he would rather pack up than join them.

Then life got easier – and more complex. People – even coarse anglers – could afford cars. Those who liked sea fishing could get to the coast more often than the one week a year at Blackpool. The big fish waters and the trout streams were within striking distance, both on the clock and with the pocket.

And that was also when the reservoirs began to open up fly fishing to a new breed of fisherman, what might well be called the coarse-fly man. The dry fly, chalk stream purist might not have been impressed with a great blank expanse of public drinking water stocked with purpose-bred rainbows. But the coarse fisherman who was kept from his sport by the close season that lasted until June, thought it was worth taking this chance to do something other than gardening for a couple of months.

Lots of them found they liked it. The mystique was removed and skills learned in the search for roach and bream stood the newcomers in good stead and, not being hidebound by unknown traditions, they found new methods that stayed within the rules.

Soon talk was of Double Taper Sevens and Pheasant Tails as well as Gozzers and Wagglers. Mind you, there were still those who felt that rearing trout, releasing them and then catching them again was about as sporting as going on a tiger hunt in London Zoo. Come to think of it, there still are.

All this change of inborn ideology and climbing out of compartments has been achieved with more than a few clashes and casualties along the way. Mostly they resulted from misunderstandings when men from different cultures and backgrounds met on the bank.

Like the gentleman who was not altogether happy about the influx on the hitherto peaceful and very lightly fished trout water he ran. 'What's he using?' he asked pointing to an angler with a plastic bucket tied round his waist with a piece of string.

Now the angler was using two things the traditionalist had never seen nor heard of. One was a shooting head which is half a fly line fixed to some stout nylon line so that when he cast, the fly line he did not have in the air to enable his rod to work would not cause unnecessary friction in the rod rings. They were a novel idea then and have become standard equipment for two good reasons – they help you cast farther and you make two fly lines for the price of one for the extra expenditure on a spool of monofilament.

The other was a line tray (in his case the plastic bucket) which stops the nylon tangling in grass or round the fisherman's feet before he 'shoots' the line.

So when the fishery manager was told the angler was using a shooting head by someone who hadn't noticed the bucket, they were immediately banned. Shooting heads were not allowed there for years in a bid to rid his mind of this awful picture of people walking round his water wearing plastic buckets, which of course they were still free to do legally if they wished.

The true story was also spread of what happened the first time it rained on the coarse-trout fraternity there. Another ban was introduced, this time on umbrellas. Someone did what he had always done when caught in a storm on the bank and put his brolly up. There was no communication; no quiet word

about 'Not here old chap' or anything of that sort. Just another rule added to the list.

Hands up all those who have ever read *all* the rules on one of the bigger trout fisheries. Well done you two! The rest of mankind has generally decided they have just paid to go fishing, not to join a library. Let's face it, in a lot of cases, if you carried right on to rule 53, section b, sub-section (ii) 'No studded waders are to be worn in the lodge between Spring Bank Holiday and the anniversary of the Battle of Bosworth west of a line from the entrance door to the glass case holding a 6lb 5oz trout caught by the chairman of the water authority in 1975' it would be within one hour of sunset and time to go home.

The upshot was, of course, that the following spring with the same determination to instil discipline into this rabble and prevent the spread of any new ideas being in evidence, a bream man trying his hand at trout fishing was ordered off the water.

'You've got an umbrella up,' he was told during a heavy shower. 'You've broken the rules so pack up and stop fishing at once.'

The trouble was, he wasn't on his own. Just around the headland was his friend. No mountaineer would have attempted to scale an overhang like that above his belt buckle without benefit of rope and experienced guides. This bulldozer of a man who had bear paws poking from his jacket sleeves where hands should have been, was not amused at the way his fishing mate had been treated. So they both packed their gear away and adjourned to the office at the lodge.

'You've just told my friend to pack up,' the conversation began.

'That's right. He had an umbrella up.' All of a sudden it sounded a bit silly.

'Well, if he goes, I go and because I wouldn't fish your highly-coloured and fatherless reservoir [not quite what he said but you get the picture] if you paid us, you'd better give us our money back.'

'I can't do that. You bought your tickets and then broke the rules.'

'Look pal. Let's put it this way. We paid to fish and you stopped us. We either get our money back or I'll take this hut down to the ground and bury you in the pieces.'

Hut! How dare he call the lodge a hut? Hold it! Swallow hard! True there were other anglers around but they seemed to have gone deaf and drifted away. Let him call the lodge what he liked.

It was clear he could take it to pieces and just as obvious that he would. So they got their money back and left with the threat of a lifetime ban ringing in their unconcerned ears.

Such incidents were fortunately rare as more willingness to compromise and forgive was shown on both sides. But they did underline the problems.

Similar disagreements occurred on the sea front with new-comers to boat fishing writing to the angling press to complain that they were being ripped off by the skippers. 'We catch them all and then we're told we can only take a couple home while the rest are sold and the money kept by the boat' was the substance of the bleat.

What they had come across was a system that had evolved as sensible all round. A couple of good fish was enough for most people and the cash raised by the fish sales helped keep the cost of the charter down. Just what they were going to do with 960lb of ling, or even how they were going to get it back to London in their Mini, was something nobody seemed to have quite worked out.

Nowadays, of course, we're much more tolerant. We all understand each other and are learning to live in complete harmony.

And if you believe that, I'd like to tell you how you can send a donation to the Preservation Trust for the Habitat of the Three Bearded Rockling.

5

Escaping Bait

THE man who goes fly fishing has one huge advantage over anglers who spend their time coarse or sea fishing – the things he uses to attract the fish are not perishable. As long as he stops the moths making a meal of materials from which his flies are tied and prevents the hooks on which they are tied from going rusty, the fly fisherman can pick up his bag and go fishing when he likes. If corrosion is avoided, spinners and spoons last for years as well.

The sea angler also has it easy in comparison with his freshwater counterpart. His lugworm may be expensive and, like fish bait, advertise its presence with a pong if left uncared for, but at least it does not escape.

The coarse angler, however, spends much of his time using bait that is not only the absolute opposite of durable, but which will disappear altogether if given half a chance.

Everyone who has tried to keep maggots knows of this propensity for wandering off on their own once your back is turned. The problem is that unless they are kept cool and dormant, all those little bodies rubbing together create heat. Once they begin to heat up a bit, they do what lots of other creatures do – they perspire. And as soon as they become the least bit sweaty and damp they can climb up anything.

Immediately it will be seen that the trouble is of the Catch 22 variety. If you leave the lid on the tin, they will sweat up more quickly and become smelly so that the fish don't fancy them as much; if you don't put the lid on the container so that the air around them can remain more fresh, they will take longer to become damp and unusable. But, if they do start to warm up a bit, they will be over the side and gone.

Refrigerators, of course, are the answer and just about

everyone who uses maggots regularly has one these days, either specially for the purpose or the one the wife believes she has for keeping eggs and milk in. This latter is fine unless you are found out and it also suffers from the handicap that you can only really get away with it if you keep the lid on the bait box while the maggots tend to keep better in the fridge without a covering.

You see what a problem it is?

Of course, before every home had an ice-box, the difficulties were far greater. Many a shed or outhouse contained tins virtually floating in shallow bowls of water for a couple of days before a big match in an effort to beat a spell of decent weather.

Now it's all done by electricity, though the poor old tackle dealer has all the inconveniences in a much multiplied form. In many cases most of the profit he should make goes in maintaining a first-class bait supply. He buys the maggots by the gallon, from each one of which he is lucky if he gets somewhere between 6 and 7 pints of saleable bait. He also needs a massive cold room or compartment to keep them in until we want them, and he has to spend hours riddling them and nursing them to perfection.

Of course, in the quantities he has to handle, they tend to get hotter more quickly as well. This not only makes it more difficult to prevent attempts to leave the premises, but adds a further debit on the cost-efficiency side, for when maggots sweat they give off ammonia – a fact that not only has a tendency towards making neighbours unfriendly but causes corrosion in the extractor units of their cold quarters. Every now and again the unit has to be replaced unless the dealer is wealthy enough to be able to afford to install a mega-expensive stainless steel one.

He also faces the dilemma that if anything goes wrong with the equipment he has a mass escape of gigantic proportions to deal with.

One dealer whom I knew well was brought as near suicide as I've ever seen anybody on the morning after his cold room had packed up during the night. He was leaning on a broom with which he had been sweeping up his bait stock from the shop floor, and eyed the wriggling little larvae swarming over everything in sight while saying, 'What a bloody mess' eight or nine times before he could even get a 'Good morning' out.

The worst of it was that he had several different sorts of bait totally integrated in their various colours which meant they would not be favoured by his clientele when he had rounded the majority of them up. As his wife ripped up the lino in the kitchen – she couldn't stand the feeling of them being flattened under it as she walked around – the hookers, pinkies and squatts climbed up rods in racks, fell from the till and headed out into the street.

You don't need as many as that to have a fine mess on your hands though. I had a friend who received complaints from neighbours as far as four doors down the street when just two pints of pinkies decided they didn't like his wash-house.

Pinkies are undoubtedly the most likely to go for a walk and are the veritable Houdinis of the maggot world. They are the larvae of the greenbottle as opposed to the hookers which are the paler but plumper offspring of the bluebottle. The other regularly used but less popular variety is the squatt which is an early housefly. He is smaller and more static than the pinkie and is loved on stillwaters because he tends to lie where he lands on the bottom instead of either burrowing into it or wandering off.

But enough of natural history.

We have established that the pinkie is a live-wire which needs to be kept at around freezing point if he is not to start crawling all over the place. Not only can he climb up walls but he can even travel across ceilings.

We were made aware of this remarkable feat on *Angling Times* when one of the staff left a tin unattended over the weekend. It was in the days before we knew chrysoidine dye could kill people and these were a nice bronze colour being much admired in their tin (with the lid off to keep them fresh, of course) on a Friday afternoon.

The gentleman concerned left in a hurry and went off to his distant fishing without them, however. Their upside-down ability was manifest on Monday morning when little orange lines made not only the walls but the ceiling look like a rather intricate map.

It was the best part of a fortnight before the odd scream stopped coming from the secretaries' office as another pinkie found its way to the dropping zone and free-fell into a type-writer through the favoured light fitting.

There is, of course, another state in which maggots are in much demand as hook bait, which is when they reach the chrysalis stage and become what anglers know and love as the caster. These go a distinct bronze colour and sink when they have just 'turned' but soon become darker and drier and floaters.

If you don't want your bait – and the interested fish – to drift off down the river, it is important to have them just right when you get to the water.

It so happened that another member of the editorial team needed ½ gallon of casters for an important match one week-end and found his source had let him down. The only answer on this hot Friday lunchtime was to buy some maggots instead and make sure they arrived at the pupa stage by Sunday morning. To speed nature on her way, he put on an electric radiator and stood the bait nearby.

Unfortunately he was then called away on urgent business. By the time he returned, the bait had been done to a turn nicely with about half the maggots giving up the ghost to become useless 'stretchers', while the remainder had sought the coolness to be found under the carpet or behind the skirting. Once again we had the problem of dealing with the result.

This time, however, the less lively hookers found suitable places in which to wait until they turned into beautiful, big bluebottles before putting in an appearance.

Soon a new sport of seeing who could down the most flies in a day with a ruler was evolved . . . but that's another story.

One of the most inspired escapes to affect me personally resulted from the provision of bait for a team representing the world's Number One angling publication. Among the chosen was Chris Dawn who was destined to become editor of *Trout*

43

Fisherman but was at that time an angling reporter. With a reputation for not getting anywhere earlier than was necessary, no one was surprised when he was not there for the share-out at the draw. He soon found the owner of the estate car where his bait had been left though.

Nobody knew he had not taken all the remaining bait until six hot hours later. The industrial sand, which is used to keep squatts in pristine condition, was still there in the large container which lay on its side. But not one of the many thousands of tiny maggots was to be seen.

It was at that time that I was teaching the owner of that particular vehicle to drive and, over the next few weeks, it became a matter of him driving us to work with me supposedly supervising but actually shooing lots of tiny flies out of the window. They came from under the carpets, out of the headlining – everywhere. To make things really spectacular he would switch on the fan and send clouds gushing round the interior.

The garage where the car was kept seemed full of them some mornings and my colleague never did explain to his neighbour's wife how she came to have a permanent colony of flies sitting admiring themselves on the mirror in her kitchen.

If maggots can cause headaches, however, there is an altogether different but equally unpleasant difficulty facing anyone who decides to try and catch predatory species by using livebait. They, too, have to be kept alive and twice I have known this practice give long-lasting offence to the olfactory organ.

The first was when a boyhood friend persuaded his granny that it would be a good idea to let him keep some fish alive overnight in her deep stone sink. With the tap left dribbling into it and the surplus water going down the overflow, all worked wonderfully. Next morning we collected the dace, gudgeon and cocky ruffe haul from the previous day's fishing, decanted them into a bucket and set out on our pike hunt.

I cannot remember what we caught, but I do know what became of one of the ruffe. It had managed to flip over the edge of the overflow pipe in that ancient sink and jam itself at the bottom. Out of sight was definitely not out of smell, however.

As the days and weeks went by, all sorts of people came and inspected the kitchen. The stink from that rotting little fish permeated throughout the house. It was a plumber who finally discovered the culprit – and got my mate treated as a leper by the rest of his family at the same time.

The second occasion was created when a road accident was narrowly averted on the way home from another piking expedition. This had been in a boat on the Broads and was much better organised. The small car was packed with two sets of gear, including all the necessary rods; an outboard engine; two oars; a large can of livebait; spare clothing . . . that sort of thing. This paraphernalia was generally rearranged when my friend stood on everything to avoid the car which hurtled in front of us. We straightened out all the contents, including ourselves, and made our way thankfully home.

About a week later my friend's wife noticed a smell in their car. He inspected it but found nothing. As the days went by the smell took over until she wouldn't go near it at all and he could only get to and from work with the windows open – rain, snow . . . whatever. He took the floor covering up, the panels off the doors . . . and then found the sticky brown gluey remains of what had been a roach tucked into the bottom of a map pocket at the back.

The distinctive odour was minimised but never eradicated. It was still there when he sold the car and, I suspect, ended up causing problems in a scrapyard somewhere in years to come.

I wonder if it's that sort of thing that people who talk about the cruelty of livebaiting have in mind?

As far as tackle is concerned there is only one piece of equipment I know of that can genuinely be considered to escape at times and, here again, it is the coarse angler who comes off worst. It is the umbrella.

A vital requirement, they make it possible for the fisherman to stay at his peg when wind and rain are doing their best to make every sensible person go home. They do need guy ropes and well secured stakes, however.

Long before I had one myself I saw an angler lose his quite spectacularly. It was during a boat match on Decoy Broad on a day when it rained so hard that everybody had to resort to using bait tins or flask tops as baling implements – it really did come down that hard. One or two enjoyed the luxury of an umbrella and it was one of these fortunates who saw his protection disappear.

A sudden gust snapped the string with which he had tied it to his boat – on the rowlock, I think. At least that sounded like what he said as the brolly turned a triple somersault as it hurtled down the wind, landed virtually on his float, and sank. The good news is that he went back on a day off during the following week and recovered it intact.

A friend with whom I fished on the Trent was not so lucky. It was a day of howling wind when pegging down was very necessary. His guys were of the home-made variety though and not up to the job. Half way through the afternoon, they parted and the brolly flipped into the river, somehow staying upside down as it scudded downstream faster than he could run beside it.

The wind was slightly across the current, too, and after about half a mile it fetched up on the far bank. The nearest bridge was about three miles upstream (of course) but before anything in the way of a rescue operation could be mounted, the errant umbrella vaulted the bank and went end-over-end across a field before finishing in a pond a few hundred yards away.

On a map from the car we traced a path that would take us to the spot. The navigation was brilliant but the umbrella was unreachable and semi-submerged. In the gathering winter dusk the only hope was an old railway sleeper which it was felt might just push it loose so that we could recapture it. As it turned out, it merely rode the brolly down and sank it totally.

The owner of the new and superior replacement needed it the following weekend when a full gale greeted a winter league match on the Great Ouse at Ely. That was the strongest wind I've ever fished in. I had the event as good as won after a couple of hours with roach coming every cast on a glass pole about

18 feet out. But that weather stopped me using the pole at all; I simply could not hold it in the teeth of that gale.

Like everyone else, I was soon legering behind my brolly as it was the only means of keeping a line in the water. The tempest continued to strengthen as the match went on and a steady stream of bait tins, buckets, mixing bowls, plastic bags and hook packets was whisked down the river. Then an umbrella came past.

My own brolly – veteran of many a blow – would not yield, but it eventually folded round me, allowing the wind to snatch a few pieces of tackle away before I could grab them.

The fellow whose back I could see downstream of me, had to do a bit of swift fielding of his own when his umbrella covering was suddenly torn to shreds. Afterwards I discovered he was one of half a dozen who had their brollies literally smashed by the wind that day.

Sometimes, when you get home and the wife says, 'You must be mad' you just don't argue about it!

6

The Lake

EVERY angler needs a place where he is sure he will be able to catch something, a spot he can go to to try out a different bait or a new piece of tackle and, even more important, somewhere to restore his confidence when things haven't been going well.

The fish don't have to be big and, of course, we know there are days when nothing feeds anywhere. But we have to have such a bolt hole to go to when we have suffered a couple of waterlickings.

It's akin to letting a miser into Fort Knox to count the bullion bars after he's had to pay his gas bill. Just such an opportunity dropped into our laps one day.

'We've got this little lake at the back of the house and we thought it would be nice to let people fish it. We don't want to sell day tickets but we thought you might know a small club who would like to rent it,' said the man on the phone who had asked for the angling editor.

The names of about a dozen clubs occurred straight away, but I was going to be implicated if cars blocked the drive or gates were left open. It would pay to be sure. In any case, securing fishing rights is like charity – it begins at home. So I told him our own little club might be interested. We really ought to have a look at it though, just to see if the fishing was any good.

The upshot was that a couple of evenings later, three of us went to try it out. While I did a circuit of the acre and a half lake to plumb the depth, the others fished. By the time I got back they were ecstatic.

'Fish a chuck,' they said. 'Roach and rudd all the time.' 'Fish up to a pound.' 'Never seen a hook.'

Breaking the record for changing tackle I had half an hour of fish committing suicide until it got dark. When we couldn't see a float any more, one of us legered to feel for bites while the other two just cast out, counted to ten then struck . . . and caught fish three times out of four.

'We're definitely interested,' I told the contact next morning. 'What are you asking for rent?'

'We thought about a pound a week,' he said, and added, 'as there's the long close season that would make it £39 a year. Is that all right?'

Was it all right?

'Well, the fishing seems pretty decent though the banks will need a bit of tidying up and one end is too shallow to be any use,' I said. 'But I'm sure the club will be pleased to help you out.'

And if they didn't want it, there were three of us who would look after it for them on our own.

That first season was terrific. Everyone who went had great fun with the beautiful rudd; roach ran to 1½lb; the odd big perch put in an appearance. The setting was superb, too. When the hall was built, a bank had been erected to dam a stream and this had formed the lake.

It was about 8 feet deep at the downstream end where the water level was controlled by a sluice, shelving to mere inches at the silted up top end.

As well as ducks, geese and a pair of resident swans, we shared the lake with several coypu. These rodents were originally introduced for their fur in the thirties but some had escaped and they were spread around Norfolk by then. It was interesting to see dad at the front and mum at the rear shepherding their infants in line-astern around the water. One old buck – if that's the word – as big as a Jack Russell and with yellow chisels for teeth, used to come and beg bread by the end of the summer.

The next winter, however, the Ministry of Agriculture waged war on the coypu. Traps were baited with sugar beet and in the cold weather they were killed in their thousands. They weren't very bright and simply packed into the wire cages as closely as they could fit.

By the spring all our coypu had gone. In their place the lake was filled by the aptly named millfoil. Clearly the coypu had not just dined on farm crops.

We worked to haul mountains of the clogging green weed on to the banks as the season approached. But the water was literally full of it. It was even smothering the lilies and ruined any hope of getting a line more than an inch or two down into the water.

The weekend before opening day, we cleared a corner behind some lilies hoping there would be some sort of gap on the Tuesday.

As luck would have it, I was the only one to be there early. Which was just as well because there was a space no more than 3 feet across left open and that was 30 feet from the bank. I plopped in a few pieces of paste, tackled up and followed them with flake on a size 10 a foot below a weighted float.

Before it cocked, the float had gone. A rudd of about ¾lb reorganised the edge of the lilies before I got him to the top, slid him across with his head up and admired his gold and scarlet livery before putting him in the net.

It was a good start that was to get better. Every cast into that hole produced a bite and not one of the rudd was much under ½lb with the biggest an immaculate 2½lb.

By the time work made me halt, I had taken fifty-five which must have weighed a total of something like as many pounds. The trouble was that that was the only catch made from the lake that year. Odd fish were caught by the very determined from the gaps they cleared in that choking weed and though we tried several times to remove enough to make a proper swim, it seemed to grow faster than we could get rid of it.

The advice we got was that we should write-off the season but cash in on the fact that the lake was perfect for the introduction and speedy growth of carp. So we went to the committee who were paying the rent and persuaded them to invest in 'a few carp'. Because there were no predators to feed on them, 4-inch fish would do and they wouldn't cost much more than another year's rent.

'After all,' we argued, 'the rent on our long lease will be wasted unless we clear the weed which could go on clogging the water indefinitely.'

So, the following January two tanks of beautiful little mirror carp were collected from the station for the icy ride into the countryside. We smashed the ice to put them into their new home after giving the temperatures of the two waters time to adjust. Though stocky and robust, they seemed so tiny to take on that mass of millfoil.

But it worked! They cropped it as it sprouted in the spring and though the carp seemed to disappear, the weed just wasn't a problem. Nobody saw the carp or caught any, but we knew what we had to thank for our fishing.

It was the September of their second season before we saw anything of them again. On a morning when just a few roach had shown, something that was definitely not another roach picked up my bread paste. It was one of those jolly little carp that I had last seen wriggling off into the icy water. But now the perfect mirror weighed 2lb 2oz.

The good news soon spread and before the winter put paid to the pleasure, a few more had been landed, the best I heard of being one of 2lb 9oz.

Leaving Norwich made me lose touch with the lake and the carp soon afterwards. A few years later, however, when on *Angling Times*, I sought permission to go back and do a feature. It was likely that with some of them (and hopefully me) catching a carp or two, pictures of them alongside ones still safeguarded of those same fish going in, would make an interesting comparison.

Though I pledged not to reveal to the world where the water was, they refused, the reasons being a bit obscure.

If they still fish it, it is likely that somebody gets broken up pretty comprehensively now and then . . . at least I hope they do. Just as I trust they're paying a good bit more than £1 a week for the privilege.

Certainly, there has never been as good a place to 'recharge my batteries' since, though there have been several other waters that have worked their confidence-restoring magic.

One was a tiny drain that yielded a few big fish but always provided a lot of little ones – until it was netted.

The first time the netting was carried out illegally. The culprits were out to make money from the sale of the fish and duly appeared in court where they were fined a derisory amount and given their nets back, presumably to go somewhere else and ruin another fishery.

Further nettings were carried out by the self same water authority who had brought the prosecution. I suppose that they were alerted to the fact that here were fish they could have for nothing. So they put them into their well-known waters where pollution and inefficient management had depleted the stocks. Anyway, my quiet 'practice ground' was destroyed and those happy fish were taken to an environment which they enjoyed so much that they disappeared for ever.

Another narrow backwater where several of us used to spend a pleasant couple of hours was subsequently filled in. It wasn't wanted to take surface water any longer, so the council used it as a tip. And the only example of that freak fish, a golden tench, it's been my joy to catch came from there.

Recently I've been delighted to have two oases in a largely fish-starved desert – both small former brick pits which are full of rudd and roach with a few tench and carp. Discovering just how big the carp are in one of them made Prince Charles's wedding a real red letter day for me too. I had got up early for a bit of relaxation before I had to set off for the Game Fair in the afternoon.

Rudd were cavorting near some reeds and I was getting my floating bread crust to them by using a bubble float half filled with water to give casting weight. It was stopped a yard up the 3lb line from a size 12 hook and the tactic was to cast well up into the wind and let the crust swing round to them.

It was unhurried fishing that was working well until this shape loomed up from the depths. A long shape it was, and I thought it was a big pike attracted by the disturbance. But the 'submarine' eased to within a foot of the surface where the sun revealed it as a truly massive carp. It didn't stop, however, but surged the final few feet to suck in the bread.

Before I could react, the line had tightened – and parted – in spite of the fact that I was using a 13ft match rod with a lot of give in the tip.

Nobody has seen a carp that big there since.

Last time I fished the other pit, fate was more kind. I did net and admire at closer quarters a 4½lb tench that tore off through the weeds on the end of my 1.1lb hook length.

They don't all get away.

7

Luck – or Confidence?

STORIES about the one that got away abound in angling circles, to the extent that the very phrase has acquired the status accorded to music hall jokes, and has come to be regarded in the same light as the image of the one-armed fisherman who was seen demonstrating to a friend the fact that he had caught one 'That long.'

Truth to tell, there are as many tales to be told about catches that have been made when it was the fish which was the unfortunate participant; incidents when the angler did everything wrong and the fish did everything necessary to lead to its escape, though it still somehow managed to end up on the bank.

If justice were to be meted out by a strict code of ethics, with catches only made when they were deserved, I suspect we would all be the worse for it – certainly the vast majority of every-now-and-again anglers would. And wouldn't it make our sport more boring if what can only be treated as an element of luck were to be removed from the reckoning?

Perhaps though, it is not really luck at all. A lot of us would be happier to put this factor of inexplicable variation down to confidence within ourselves rather than to some external force over which we have no control. Joseph Conrad was almost certainly right when he heard a Frenchman speaking of luck say 'or as the English call it, Providence, because they like to have God on their side'. We can all recall instances when we knew things were going to go well before we ever got out of bed; when we were certain of a good peg before we put our hand in the bag at the draw.

Anyone who has match fished regularly knows there are the days, or at times a whole series of days, when you dread picking a number. Wherever it is, you know there won't be much to catch and that the whole thing will be one uncomfortable embarrassment.

Then there are the good runs when you know you can pick an end peg, or any other spot you like. You could almost tell the steward the peg to write your name against before you have drawn it.

Confidence, that's the key, that feeling of complete belief in your method, your bait, your gear and your judgement. The cornerstone is that faith in your ability which lets you know that your ideas will work, whereas – on those dour occasions – you tend to sit it out with things as they are because of a deep-down awareness that whatever you try isn't going to make any difference.

Perhaps that is why opening days of new seasons are often occasions to remember with affection when looking back over the years. The enforced lay-off has a beneficial effect in several ways:

There is the psychological one that comes from having had time for the good days to have become dominant in the mind so that the confidence-sapping, fishless ones, while not necessarily forgotten, are ignored;

There is the thought-concentrating advantage that comes from having had time during those water-starved days to get the painting, digging and shopping chores out of the way so that uncluttered attention can be devoted to the important matter in hand;

Allied to this is the fact that, unable to fish, the angler has time to prepare his tackle to a pitch of perfection it will not attain for a further twelve months. For this one time in the year, the fisherman knows where everything is in his tackle box or fishing bag. All his tackle is new or freshly cleaned and prepared so that it can be totally trusted. And the bait or flies have been lovingly tended in a way that is quite impossible when the angler could actually be fishing instead of fussing over them.

Every time the ending of the close season is discussed, a mass of anglers say they want it to remain. I suspect it is only because so many of us know we would never get things into this perfect state of readiness at all if we did not have to find a substitute to satisfy the craving when we can't go fishing.

How they stand out, those sixteenths of June! Those April days when the first fly lands in front of unwary trout! Those mental video recordings show flash-backs of a net of rudd so vivid that Walt Disney could not have made them sparkle more; the only pure golden tench I've ever caught glistening in the early sunlight of midsummer; 120 fish before having to leave off and go to work; five tench putting in an appearance in time for breakfast; and my son's dawn bream of 3½lb.

That confidence can be there on other occasions, too. A classic example was an open match when I drew in an awkward section to fish but one where I knew bream could be found. No one could have bought that peg for anything and once I got to my spot it was upstream of a whole stretch of unfishable bank that had not been pegged at all. An hour before the start I had that match as good as won.

My strategy was to put some good, pongy bait out filled with maggots which would drift gently down into the unfished length and entice everything to move in front of me. For an hour I forced myself to leave that magic spot alone while settling for small fish under my feet.

First cast to that far bank holding area produced the expected twitch of the quivertip, followed by the steady bending of the indicator. The bream was not big, but nicely over the pound. It was what I had anticipated . . . not big enough to cause any concern over breakage or undue strain on the hook-hold, but lovely, weight-building potential of the kind that promised a lot of them around.

There were not many fish about, however, but by the end I had had eight bites which put eight bream on the scales for a total of 11½lb. It was not an unbeatable weight, but I would have been shattered if I had not won on one of those rare days when nothing had gone wrong. As it happened the second man had 6lb-odd.

That certainty that what you are doing is right can work with specimen fish, too. I used to know one water that never produced the big bream I had convinced myself it must hold, though it was only the odd report of tackle being smashed unaccountably that led me to this conclusion. My ultimate decision was that these bigger fish must only feed regularly outside daylight hours when few people ever fished there with adequate tackle.

It led to a lot of fun in perfecting the right way to set about them. I did not want a lot of the more usual buzzing and bleeping and blinking indicators beloved by the after-dark, big-fish brigade, but something 'on the rod'.

Now most butt bite indicators suffer from one big drawback, a failing inherent in their basic concept. That is that you have to point your rod straight at the bait to make them efficient. The obstacle is on the strike. If you think about it, it is obvious that moving the rod upwards or sideways from the straight-out position means a lot of line has to be drawn sideways or upwards against the resisting water before the rod reaches an angle where a big fish can make it bend. If fish are biting daintily, like those suspected, soft-mouthed old bream were expected to do, you have a built-in danger point where the hook can pull out while the line is pretty-well straight.

So I used a swingtip with a Betalite glowing at the end only to discover that after a relatively short time looking at this one point of light in the darkness, my eyes began to play tricks. Movement that was not there was imagined while I missed the real thing. The answer was to have a second light spot to act as a reference point.

This was provided by a second Betalite taped on top of the rod at a point where it was just about in line with the tell-tale swingtip light. By lining them up, it was easy to see the least twitch just as well as it would show in broad daylight. It worked so well that it is a method I would recommend to anyone. Chuck all those weird and wonderful gadgets away!

The belief in waiting until after dark to go for the fish no one contacted in matches worked, too. Bream like dustbin lids came from pre-baited swims on a stretch of river that did not yield more than the odd bream over a pound normally. The best recorded in ordinary circumstances was under 3½lb compared with the biggest in darkness of well over 5½lb. It was having the confidence to try the unusual which triumphed. Luck had little to do with it.

A case where doing something out of the ordinary brought about a much more valuable reward was when that fine Midland matchman, Joe Brennan, won the Gladding Masters. The match was staged at the National Watersport Centre at Holme Pierrepont near Nottingham in the days before it had developed into the top-class coarse fishery it was to become.

Half way through the five-hour contest, there were some anxious people around. In front of quite a gallery, nobody had had so much as a sucked maggot. Joe saved the prize money having to be shared out in an undignified draw, by taking a couple of pike he knew were present. A big lobworm tweeked across the bottom did the trick for him with only one other fish being caught by the assembled cream of the country's match aces.

Some put it down to luck. I believe, however, it was really that other phenomenon at work – a man who was on top of his form thinking out a way of beating the conditions and having the nerve to do something totally at odds with what everyone had come expecting to do.

Mind you, there are occasions when a happening that can be regarded as nothing short of fortuitous accounts for an outstanding catch. Like the time when an open match on a Fenland drain was won with a huge catch due to a complete fluke. The eventual winner had not had a bite from his carefully baited far-bank swim for an hour. Then a boat – rare for that water – came down the stretch and made him pull his float tackle out of the way.

While it was at his rod end waiting for the craft to go by, the float disappeared and the angler was astonished to find himself playing a good bream. Without putting in a drop of bait to hold them, he took fish after fish from that stationary shoal for the next four hours to weigh in more than 90lb, which was about ten times more than he needed to secure victory. Virtually every bream in the whole area was congregated under his feet. And if that boat had not come past, he would never have known.

There are other fish that would never be landed if everything went according to the rule book. Like the big carp taken in a winter league match by my friend John Anderson – but which couldn't be weighed in. The event was on the north bank of the River Nene below Peterborough where more than one man has been frightened by the odd massive carp that crops up there from time to time.

John hooked one of them on his 1½lb line towards the end of the contest, the rules of which stated that an angler had a quarter of an hour after the final whistle to land any fish he hooked during the match. John needed a lot longer than that. While he followed the fish down the bank, the rest of his catch was weighed in along with everyone else's. He just went on playing that fish.

'Break off. You can't weigh it in anyway,' he was advised by several departing fishermen as they packed their gear and headed for home in the gathering darkness.

'No fear,' said John, 'I'm going to beat this. It's the biggest fish I've ever had on.' The gallery dwindled to a few friends whose torchlight guided him along the river as he stuck to the task of keeping in touch with the unseen monster which led him nearly half a mile along the bank.

Eventually, against all the odds, he brought it in close enough to be netted. If memory serves me right, it weighed just over 24lb – enough to have won the match for the team as well as for John himself. But, of course, it didn't count.

An even unluckier fish was a salmon caught by another friend of mine who is much addicted to the species. On a trip north, Peter Naylor, advertisement manager of *Trout and Salmon*, purchased a new fly line. Finding the water in perfect condition, he admits he took a chance by simply knotting it on to the backing line so that he could get on to the water quickly. Who would want to take the time to join it to the nylon properly?

Of course, the inevitable happened. Murphy's Law – or Sod's Law if you prefer – which is well known to engineers, is true for fishing as well, for if something can go wrong it will do so at the worst possible moment. Peter was soon into a fish of worthy proportions which tore off in the fast current until the 'temporary' knot hit the tip ring. Something had to give – and it was the knot. The result was that the salmon took the new line away with it. In the circumstances, it had to be a sinker.

However, later in the day, Peter dragged in the fly line and began to wind it up. At least he had the line back, even if he had lost the fish, he thought. Then the line began to move off . . . The salmon was still attached.

Sportsman that he is, he threaded the line back down the rod, tied it to the backing again and set about playing the luckless fish a second time. All went well and he landed it. I believe it weighed 18lb.

Not that we are always that lucky. The biggest ever tench I hooked in a river I fished a lot at one time decided to take a single pinkie on a size 24 and ¾lb line fished on a pole. One half his size would have caused problems but this one looked close on 5lb. I did not interfere with his intention of visiting the nearest weedbed for long!

Perhaps even more galling was sitting next to an angler who won a match with more than 16lb of bream while I couldn't get a bite of any sort. For more than three hours, he took a steady succession of fish which refused to move on to my bait. He said afterwards that it was as if there had been a wall across the water. My only solace was that the man on the other side of him weighed in nothing either.

Fish you can't catch can be even more disheartening than that, however – when you can see them. One day at Draycote Reservoir, I moved after taking a couple of stockies and, in a corner near some stones, found an angler fishless and preparing to move though the water in front of him was virtually boiling with fish that were splashing and apparently actively feeding.

'I'm going before they drive me mad,' he said. 'I've done everything I can think of for hours and gone through my fly box without having a touch. You give 'em a go.'

So, for about two hours, I did. It would have been possible to foul hook a fish or two if I had tried, there was such a concentration of them in that relatively small, sheltered piece of water. But they wouldn't look at anything I had to offer though they were active the whole time.

When I, in my turn, became dispirited to the point that I was glad to move away, another angler stepped gladly into the fray. During the day, at least four of us fished that corner and not one of us took a fish. Trout can, of course, be like that but I've never seen so many of them virtually thumbing their noses with their fins at one time. Hand grenades, that was the only solution any of us could suggest.

Of course, sometimes we do make problems for ourselves. I recall seeing one man playing a fish when the reel detached itself from his rod handle. In his surprise he dropped it so that it could bounce down the bank before plopping into the river. The small fish was landed by the angler handlining the nylon through the rod guides. Then he had to recover the reel from the water which was too deep for him to reach it with his landing net. A couple of hundred yards of line were pulled from the spool before the reel came up on the end of it.

An even more head-scratching predicament was created by another angler of my aquaintance at the start of a match where he had such a comfortable piece of bank that he decided to sit in a folding chair. When the whistle sounded, he went to make his first cast, only to discover that the line went round the leg under his canvas seat. It was not from reel to first ring which would have been easy to put right that was looped under him either, but between butt and second ring. This meant he had to take everything to bits and start again with hoots of laughter from his 'friends' providing an accompaniment.

Probably the worst thing that can happen to an angler, however, is that he loses a good fish and knows that there was nothing he could have done to prevent it; when he has done everything right and still seen it swim away. Maybe that really is luck running against you.

One 'fish of a lifetime' that was lost like that was in a tiny Fenland drain, one of many that run for miles largely unfished through the flat fields. This one was no more than 25 feet wide, from 2½ to 3 feet deep, and full of lilies. It was fished a bit by

local lads behind a pumping station that sucked the water out of it in winter, but 'fishermen' generally ignored it.

A couple of us discovered, however, that a farmer's wife living in an isolated house on its banks was keeping ducks on a stretch of it. They were preventing weed growing and making the water coloured; there had to be fish there! We obtained permission to fish it and had good sport throughout one summer. As winter approached, we tried for pike, too, and had several fish into double figures.

Then I hooked something that was far bigger. The absolutely massive pike surfaced once as it swirled round, seeming to be even longer due to the confined water it lived in. The snout was like a dinner plate as the huge head emerged just before the pike rolled over and 'coughed' the hooks out. I have seen other pike do the same thing in ejecting a bait and hooks. Coughing is the only way to describe how they clear their throats of the obstruction.

As I say, there was nothing else I could have done. The strike was timed as well as any attempt to set hooks into a pike's bony jaw can be, for there is always an element of doubt; there was no undue pressure; there was no slack line. It was just that the pike won. And it was the biggest fish I have ever tangled with, albeit briefly, in fresh water.

There was an interesting sequel to that encounter, for the following spring a couple of locals and some visiting gentry appeared in the magistrates' court for netting that drain and illegally removing fish for sale. After they were fined their £10 or something equally fatuous for ruining our sport – an offence certainly worthy of restoring the death penalty for – I heard from one of them how they had come across what I was sure must have been 'my' pike.

They used to stake their net across the drain, then go well upriver and drive everything down towards it. On one sweep, the net was already tightened by several fish when something huge hit it and broke right through.

'Bust a hole clear through the net,' he said. 'Must have been some pike to do that.'

It was, too! I would have known just how big, if only I had hooked it on one of those lucky days.

8

Trout Fishing and Fly Tying

TROUT fishing and fly tying are so interwoven that you won't find a magazine on the game aspect of angling that doesn't devote a fair proportion of its space to the flies themselves.

Like many others I suspect, it was the dressing of flies which drew me to this facet of angling in the first instance. I had made all sorts of tackle, including rods, but the final accolade would obviously be to catch a trout on something I had concocted myself.

Several anglers had told me that the greatest thrill was to see a fly you have dressed yourself sipped in by a fish who has mistaken it for one of the natural insects he is feeding on. It is true, too, though that seeing gnats trying to mate with pieces of fur and feather you have tied to a hook can be a real mark of approbation as well!

I read every book on the subject in the local library at the time and thank Heaven there is a wider choice of better literature on the subject now. Those volumes were obviously written purely for fly fishermen and, as a bare beginner, I had no idea what most of the patterns were supposed to do. Most of the instruction assumed far too much of the novitiate as well.

The result was that a winter of fiddling produced a few half-decent flies and the following spring I practised my casting with a borrowed rod. It must have worked a bit because I caught my first rainbow which weighed less than 4oz and had wandered from a private stretch downstream of where the water was being thrashed with the fly line.

It was not until years later, however, that I was inveigled into dabbling with the fly again. But, once more, I soon decided to stick to coarse fishing, even selling the assortment of trout flies I had accumulated, mostly my own ham-fisted creations, for £1.50. And the very next weekend somebody caught a 5lb brownie from Grafham on one of them. C'est la vie!

It was only when John Wilshaw, subsequently to become editor of both *Trout Fisherman* and *Trout and Salmon*, moved to *Angling Times* and came to live near us that I really got to grips with the fly rod. He taught me more about fly tying in one evening than I had discovered from reading in years and it has been as much a therapy as a hobby ever since.

In return I showed him some chub haunts on the Welland. First time out he had several with the best topping 5lb. I wish I had benefitted from his fly fishing/fly tying tuition to the same extent.

The trouble, I think, is that in common with many another coarse-cum-trout man I'll never feel for the trout in the same way that I do for the roach and the tench. Perhaps the secret is in starting young enough.

In truth, I have always likened fly fishing to running a race in which you erect your own hurdles just in case you should get to the finish too fast. For, although they can learn surprisingly quickly, trout are basically stupid fish. If, as Walton claimed, chub are the fearfullest of fishes, trout can be the dimmest.

The pugnacious tendencies of the rainbow in particular often make him bite at anything entering his domain out of nothing more than sheer nastiness whether he intends eating it or not, a trait of which many lure designers have made good use. Without the protection given by the rules, which vary from water to water, numbers could soon be depleted. Hence those 'hurdles'.

To tempt a trout with a fly is certainly not the best practical means of catching them with a rod. It is an art form in which the first man-made hurdle to be scaled is that you cannot use a weight to give casting distance. That must come from timing the catapulting action of a lively rod which is bent by the force through the air as much as by the weight of the heavy line itself.

And then the fly presents a barrier. Perfect patterns can be bought and books are full of other dressings which can be tied in such a multiplicity of ways that it is a complete muddle for the beginner. Although presentation is probably more vital than the fly selection a lot of the time, the difference between a size 14 and a size 10, or a touch of scarlet, or a flash of silver in the fly's make-up, can mean the difference between success and failure.

And a further obstacle on some running waters is that it is only permitted to cast upstream and not run an offering down to the quarry which seems the natural and obvious thing to do by a stick-float trained addict.

The coarse angler turning to trout finds that many of the skills he has learned which are vital when trying to catch as much as he can from the swim in front of him – often within a limited time span – are now taboo. He cannot groundbait or use natural baits. He must use only artificial lures, which were the very things not allowed in his match days, and sometimes only those that float. When the trout are playing hard to catch his hands are tied.

Of course there are exceptions to every rule and there are areas, strangely enough the traditional fly fishing parts of these islands, where the townies come out to join the country youngsters with worms and minnows to hammer as many fish as they can for the table (or the market). But that is not fly fishing.

Rather, fly fishing is a contradiction. It is at the same time the most demanding and yet the easiest; the most rewarding and the most infuriating; the most artificial and yet the part of the sport where a knowledge of the fish's natural world is of greatest advantage.

Demanding because, whereas in most types of angling a novice can lollop a line into the water any-old-how and catch something, in fly fishing a degree of skill must be acquired before there can be any consistent success; and the easiest because when the trout are feeding they can be so careless as to pretty well give themselves up.

Rewarding because dedication and an attention to the minutest detail can bring a fish on a day when the unthinking fail; and infuriating due to the fact that there are times when even the most polished of practitioners cannot make any of the fish avidly feeding in front of him give a second glance to anything he offers.

Artificial because the vast majority of the trout we catch are put there specially for that purpose, so much so that you often have a fair idea of what size of fish you are likely to hook; but natural for the reason that it is the area of angling where an understanding of that underwater existence which is the life of the fish, gained over years of quiet observation, can yield the richest return.

It is also unfortunate that fly fishing suffers from what amounts to a necessary evil – the limit. This ceiling on what may be caught is against the real feeling of all angling but it is difficult if not impossible to avoid if the river or lake is not to be wrecked by the depletion of its stock on those occasions when the fish are grabbing anything, however it is hurled in their direction.

The trouble is that the limit, be it a brace or eight, sets a target in the angler's mind. It is easy to see why so many drive themselves to attain the magic number. In our commercial age it seems only sensible to catch the maximum permitted number for your outlay. Obviously the more you take away the more it reduces the price per fish and it also presents a solid argument which the non-angling public (probably including the wife in most cases) will understand, and that can be useful when you want to go again.

The danger is that it can become paramount to the angler as well. Several of the better known trout writers have built reputations on their ability to catch the limit regularly which, in turn, leads to a remarkable cumulative tally they can declare at the end of the season.

So often it seems that the reaction of others to his catch becomes more important than any benefit or enjoyment the angler feels within himself. Not that I believe most of the men at the top don't fulfil themselves; it is just that so many others who are trying to emulate them will not reap the full benefit from their days by the water. A man can have a potentially great time only to go home feeling that he has failed in some way just because he was one off that limit. How sad it is.

An idea to be recommended is that used at fisheries like that at Narborough in Norfolk. There a nominal sum is paid for the day's use of the facilities with any and all fish caught being weighed in and paid for by the pound when the angler leaves. As the water is stocked daily, the fishmongers among us can be sure of a hefty bag – together with a bill to match. Those who want to try out a new pattern are sure fish will see it, for it makes sense for the fishery to keep the stock level high. Anyone intent on seeking out bigger fish can do it without the fear that he has spent a considerable amount of money for nothing if he fails. And the purist who wants to pick a few fish off the top can do that, too.

The way people are generally encouraged to catch fish (and that is certainly not something that can be said of every trout water) makes it another of those confidence restoring places, somewhere to revive the faith in yourself that fades after a series of blanks. It also makes such waters the ideal places to start a youngster off.

Take warning, though, from one angler whose infant prodigy was enjoying himself there. 'My dad will be pleased with me,' he said proudly, displaying a bulging bag with what must have been getting on for thirty trout in it. I hope his dad, who was fishing out of sight well down the bank, had his cheque book with him.

9

Close Encounters

'STUDY to be silent,' Walton said, and his advice has been instilled in generation after generation of anglers ever since. It is difficult to achieve in some situations, however.

I don't imagine for a minute that Izaak envisaged that twentieth-century anglers, trying to find the same satisfaction that he enjoyed by the water, would have to time their casts to coincide with gaps between a virtual convoy of boats on some rivers in the summer.

I am sure, too, that he would have been appalled at the prospect of eight men trying to catch cod or whiting while sharing 5 feet of pier rail on a dark, winter's night.

So much give and take has to be shown in some of these situations that the serene contemplation often associated with our sport sometimes seems to have gone out of fashion along with the flax line and the greenheart rod.

By the very nature of things, there has to be a certain amount of friction between anglers and the boating fraternity. It can be kept at a reasonable level, but it is not always easy when the antics of some of the Sunday Sinbads is called into question. When discussing the inherent animosity in the sharing of water with one of their number recently, it was clear he could see no reason for my disquiet at what he and his fellows were planning to do to yet another piece of water they intended 'opening up'.

'Let me put it like this,' I said in attempting to help him see the problem from the angler's standpoint. 'Suppose we decided to start a model torpedo club on the river, wouldn't you be a bit concerned at sailing through that stretch when we were trying out our creations, possibly every Sunday morning which is your favourite time of the week?'

I think he began to see the logic. He certainly did not welcome the suggested introduction when I pointed out that there was probably as much reason for us to worry about his boats as there was for him to fear the torpedoes.

One stretch which I fished regularly had the benefit of a rowing club not far along the bank. Their eights hurtling up and down the river now and then was an understandable nuisance and something we could live with. Truth to tell it was almost certainly a case of their upsetting us more than they did the fish.

What was much more difficult to endure was the megaphone-aided idiot who would insist on dashing about around them like some agitated mother hen in a rubber dinghy which was p elled by an oversized outboard engine. We did not get around to stringing some hefty nylon across the water to decapitate him, though it was discussed none-too-light-heartedly on several occasions.

Then there was my unfortunate friend in a match on the boat-choked Norfolk Broads. We all put up with the cruisers churning up and down and we even kept our calm as day launches nipped in and out of the reeds in an apparent attempt to snaffle the tackle of the unwary. It was when this sailing craft, manned by an utter incompetent, arrived in his swim that his love for his fellow man was streched to the limit.

The yacht tacked back and forth across the river directly in front of him in a bid to head upstream into the stiff wind. Everyone but the occupant could see that he was never going to make it. At each reach across the river – causing consternation to lots of cruisers in the process – he left it a little later to jib, hoping this would gain him an extra fraction on the way to his goal. It didn't!

In the end, the inevitable happened. He left it too late, and it was only my mate's athletic leap which prevented him being run down by the boat. As it was, his net was flattened and a lot of tackle well-mangled. That helmsman was asked in no uncertain terms if he had now got it into his head that he had only one way to go?

After a similar experience on the Welland, a member of a

northern angling club planned his next trip there very carefully. The local yacht club had a stretch to use which anglers fished at their peril, but a buoy marked the limit of sailing with fishermen left in peace above it . . . except for this one sailor who made a habit of going where he liked upriver. It was he the Yorkshireman was prepared for.

When the dinghy sailed through his swim, he put down his coarse rod, picked up a beachcaster and hurled a heavy lead draped with big treble hooks right into the offending sails. Once the hooks had snagged solidly, he leaned back in a well-muscled strike and ripped several hundred pounds worth of Terylene from top to bottom. The matelot was not amused, but decided a landing to seek retribution was not a good idea when he realised the offender was accompanied by a busload of colleagues who were not altogether upset by what had happened. Desperate situations do sometimes call for desperate measures after all!

It may not be the sort of behaviour the followers of the Gentle Art would like to become noted for and, while we would not all condone the action, at least we can understand the feelings that led to it happening.

The same can be said of the virtual 'war' that nearly broke out on one of the Broads on a peaceful Sunday morning. A match that had begun early to avoid the disturbance sure to be encountered later in the day, was in progress when the local faction of the Territorial Army arrived intent on using the same area for an assimilated water-borne landing. It was perhaps unfortunate for them that several of the anglers had been in a proper war not many years previously and decided that they would bring old skills into use to 'repel' the invasion. It was only thanks to the fact that the officer in charge of the landing force had enough sense to beat a hasty retreat in order to find somewhere else to play, that he did not lose a fair proportion of his troops!

Among sea anglers, it often seems to be that the fishermen have difficulty in coming to terms with others who are out to fish the same spot. Close-packed boat fishing, of course, calls for considerable forbearance from all involved and, though tangles are not infrequent, the problems are normally sorted out amicably. Which is something that cannot always be said of altercations on piers and jetties.

Here's how one clumsy angler lost his tackle on a dark and damp Saturday night – always a good time not to fish a popular pier if you can avoid it. He had come to try his luck with his pike gear pressed into sea service and slung a weight out over several other lines in his bid to catch a cod. One of the properly equipped regulars had a bite soon afterwards and began to haul in a fish of 5 or 6lb while the newcomer remained huddled in the warmth of the shelter on the pier.

It was as the cod was within a few feet of the rail, that he suddenly noticed his rod top 'knocking' as it had been the whole time the fish was being winched aloft. The result of his charge forward and sweeping strike was that he knocked the cod off the hook and back into the sea.

Realising what he had done and recognising its seriousness mirrored in the other fisherman's eyes, he began to offer an apology which concluded with the words, 'I won't do it again.'

'You certainly won't tonight,' was all the veteran said as he took the startled pike man's rod and threw it over the side.

Due to the pressure on space, such stern measures, though thankfully rare, are not entirely unknown. One regular on a noted pier was known by his fellows for the way he dealt with anyone casting their line over his. A big man who could get away with such things, his answer was simply to produce his bait knife and cut the offending line. As far as I know, he is still doing it.

Another famous angler who had his own way of making sure he fished in 'his' spot was Sam Hook of Lowestoft. Sam held the cod record for years with a fish he caught from what was known appropriately as Cod Corner at the end of the Claremont Pier. Whoever and however many were fishing there, Sam would tackle up and cast over the top of the lot of them before walking through to place his rod where he always put it. Not many people could get away with a stunt like that, but the local tackle dealer was pretty well regarded as part of the pier's structure.

An old-timer who frequented another pier had a much more subtle way of clearing the rail. His trick also livened up things during waiting periods at the wrong stage of the tide. He would cautiously place his foot on the butt of a rod stuck out over the side and give it a firm push. This, of course, had the effect of making the tip jump up and down so that the owner would see the 'bite', grab his rod and strike at it.

By the time he had realised he had 'missed' it, he would find our old friend's rod fishing happily where he had always put it.

We are supposed to be a gregarious lot, we anglers, but there are limits to just how close we want to be to our fellows – even fellow anglers. It's probably just as well the rules make match-men sit a minimum of 20 yards apart!

10

All at Sea

'HOW would you like a week's free shark fishing in the Mediterranean?' came the invitation, literally out of the blue.

The odds against any angler turning down such an offer are about the same as you'd get if you wanted to back your milkman's float in the Monaco Grand Prix. To make things even better, the dates did not interfere with any commitments; I had a week's holiday due; and it was in November when you're not exactly looking forward to the best of the weather in England.

The offer came from the Shakespeare tackle company who had run some successful fishing weeks for Fred Pontin whose travel company also owned hotels in Torremolinos. He wondered if shark fishing was an attraction that could be added to the list of activities he could offer his guests on the Costa del Sol and had asked Shakespeare to find out.

They organised a quartet of fact-finders and when one of them had to drop out at the last minute I grabbed the chance to fill the gap.

We followed the lead of that indomitable westcountry big fish catcher, Mike Millman, who was aided and abetted by Ray Baker, their sales manager at the time. In spite of their experience all over the world, we failed to catch a single shark in four days afloat. We did have one run but whatever it was bit off the four pilchards I had on for bait and departed.

We did boat all sorts of smaller fish, including some brilliant golden 'dorado', and a big octopus escaped by walking away under the boat when it was scared rather than gaffed by a gormless deckhand.

We had our doubts about the skipper too. Real seamen have

a sixth sense about where they are as well as where fish are to be found that amazes the landlubber. I have been on crab boats that went straight to pot markers three miles offshore in morning mist so thick and disorientating that I couldn't have told which way the beach was. And when I asked Shrimp Davies why he didn't use the thousands of pounds worth of electronic gear on Cromer lifeboat much, he simply said, 'There's eleven fathoms under us here,' and switched on. He was right, but he wasn't finding the depth, he was checking the equipment. He only needed it in waters well away from his own backyard.

Skippers you can trust are like that and Mike knows a lot of them. 'This guy isn't sure where we are, never mind the fish,' he muttered as our captain pored over his charts half an hour out of harbour on a sparkling blue sea with crystal-clear visibility.

Any misgivings about him were cleared up the following spring when Shakespeare organised a tackle dealers' seminar on the same stretch of the Spanish coast. Sharking was on the agenda, as it should have been a better time of year to pick some up. Sixty people said they would like to go. In spite of arrangements made well ahead, the boat was still out of the water on the first day.

The original ten couldn't go but reorganisation on an amicable basis cut the number to fifty for the five remaining days.

Day by day, however, the message kept coming back along the coast, 'The boat will be ready tomorrow.' By the time the last twenty had to be reduced to a final ten for the sole trip left with no one actually having set foot on board, a proper draw was the only answer. Half the participants were naturally disappointed with the others delighted.

The lucky ones were seen off the following morning. At last somebody was going to have a try for those elusive shark. But they came back madder than ever for, in spite of the eighty-mile round trip, the fact that the engine wouldn't start had meant the boat had stayed in harbour again.

We did however find some great sport with light tackle from the rocks and harbour walls down there. You had to watch your bait though. Mike Millman and I were busy accusing each other of nicking neatly cut up squid on one occasion when I spotted a ginger tabby disappearing into the rocks with another mouthful. Apparently cats live wild in some of the sea walls and thought their need was greater than ours.

Many of the locals use long poles with line that lets the hook come straight to hand, but British coarse gear works well, too, for a whole aquarium of beautiful fish that feed around every one of the T pieces and 'banjos' that make the beaches such a bather's paradise. There are some ugly specimens as well that nobody seems inclined to handle, so it pays to be careful.

It is great fun in the sunshine and more than once since I've enjoyed angling next to some of the local ladies who are getting a tan in their bikinis while they fish. It's got to be better than hiding behind a windbreak and warming your hands on a hurricane lamp next to a big hairy fellow wearing eight layers of woollies.

But the macho man who writes off all angling with an offhand 'It's OK for older blokes, I suppose, but I like something more active myself' has clearly never been introduced to British sea fishing.

For here is a sport that can demand all the muscle-stretching activity anyone can handle and provide 'laying-it-on-the-line' thrills as well if you want to include scaling dangerous cliff faces and getting into tide races in small boats as part of the pastime.

Sea anglers around our shores need to be fit, not in the gentle jogging sense but more in the decathlon meaning of the word. They have to have strength and endurance for use in a variety of ways.

For instance, if you intend casting your lead weight nearer Denmark than anyone else's from an east coast cod beach, co-ordination of trained muscle akin to that exhibited by a pole vaulter is required. In this case, however, it is the tackle at the other end of the pole which is sent into space rather than the athlete himself.

If dinghies are to be launched from the beach, then the ability looked for in a weightlifter is handy. Unless you like that type of physical challenge, all the enjoyment of the time afloat is tempered by the sure knowledge that the sort of effort which only used to be required of the coalman's horse awaits you. And you will be expected to do it on mud and sliding stones, not a nice, firm road.

If you aspire to join the fraternity who light up the coastline for miles on dark winter nights, you have to have the sort of stamina exhibited by the attack forces in the Falklands. The first loads carried through the energy-sapping banks of moving shingle are nothing to do with the fishing itself. They are composed of windbreaks, braziers, lamps, chairs, beds, sacks of coke, cooking utensils, water containers and enough food to withstand an average-duration siege.

Once an encampment of a permanence that would require planning permission anywhere else has been established, the fishing tackle can be brought in on a second trek. As well as being bigger, stronger and a good deal heavier than the equipment used by followers of the other angling disciplines, sea tackle has one other ingredient that makes it totally unsuited to long trudges along the shore – the weights.

Whereas fly fishermen tend not to use them at all; spinning men to have a few Wye leads; and coarse anglers to carry a lot of little weights that add up to not a lot, the beach man needs something that will stay put in a 10-knot tide. This means an assortment of aerodynamically designed lumps of lead weighing anything from ¼ to ½lb apiece, either purchased specially or cast by the angler himself from the melted down flashing from any convenient roof.

Many more than will actually be used have to be carted to the base camp. Usually a few are lost in wrecks, rocks or tangled masses of gear left there by other anglers the previous weekend. Others are set free when the line parts as a multiplying reel stops rotating, usually because the line has got into an irretrievable, knotted bird's nest. A bird's nest is that accumulation of waste monofilament nylon which clogs the entire bottom of the rod when line comes off the spool faster than it is going out through the rings, usually because the weight has stopped, though the reel doesn't know this and goes gamely on turning. Once seen, the reason for the name is obvious.

The first time this jams up the reel near the start of a cast and causes what is known as a crack-off, the novitiate beachcaster can easily believe he has broken every casting record ever set as he watches in awe as his terminal tackle streaks towards the horizon. In fact, though he has cast his lead farther than he ever has before and probably ever will do again, the joy is short-lived when he finds he is no longer connected to it.

Sometimes the line does not part when a reel jams and this can be even worse as well as extremely dangerous. One man on the east coast discovered this when his boat colleague's lead swung round instead of outwards at high speed and re-arranged his teeth for him. The force involved can be gauged from another instance in which a 5oz lead became so deeply embedded in a building at the end of a pier as it spun round that a knife had to be used to pry it free. A second angler, whose head had been within a foot of the point of impact turned very white and shook like a leaf in a gale when he realised what could have happened to his good looks.

Jamming reels connected to hefty weights can cause other problems as well. I remember a man who had just taken up fishing arriving with his gear on Cromer Pier. He was shown how to cast by one of the helpful locals who unfortunately forgot to disengage the spool on the strange reel so that line would be paid out. The result was that when he gave a demonstratory swing, the rod followed the weight, leaping from his hands to disappear into the waves. Only his prompt offer to replace the equipment prevented his following closely behind.

Perhaps it is the beach fisherman more than any other who suffers most from the 'You should have been here yesterday' syndrome. Word of fish coming inshore travels like wildfire among the brotherhood of the coast so there is always a real possibility of being in the right place but a tide or two too late.

I recall one cod trip in just such circumstances. I had not only been told of but seen pictures of a couple of catches that had been made the day before and when I hooked something that really pulled with the tide, I thought that the daddy of them all had waited for me. It took a lot of pumping and heaving before I brought my catch into the surf some way down the beach. It was enormous all right. Two of us couldn't lift it and had to drag it up the shingle.

It was a waterlogged foam mattress long past the luxury yacht stage.

I once hooked a real fish that took as much effort to subdue on a day after skate off north Norfolk. We caught mackerel on the way out to the bank the skipper had told us about, and these fresh offerings were taken steadily by the thornback rays so that we all had good sport with fish between 10 and 18lb. Looking like something left over from a nightmare, the fish were giving us a memorable day.

When the tide began to flood, I let my pound of lead trundle along to find a slack spot where one of the skate might be lying. My bait was picked up by something 40 feet down and 70 yards away. Playing these fish is always akin to flying a kite under water, but this was really hard work. I could not control it at first and it took a good ten minutes with everyone getting excited before I hauled a skate of 12½lb to the surface . . . backwards.

While everyone else went back to their fishing, I winched it slowly alongside until the skipper could finally gaff it. As he did so, the hook fell out. It is not uncommon for thornback to pick up a hook in their long, spiky tails but I found out why it is rare to actually catch one the wrong way round.

Anglers are not the only ones who are tuned in to pick up the coastal news, though, and within a week a trawler headed north out of Lowestoft had scraped the bank clean and ruined the sport.

Reports of good catches lead to clubs arranging matches at venues that are producing fish as well, and one I knew of decided to fish an over-night match at Orfordness. This is a shingle bank just off the Suffolk coast that is reached by boat. To fish the tide over, virtually means being marooned out there with a boat coming to collect the anglers in the morning. The trouble for one of these fishermen on this winter night was that he had developed a tummy bug during the day but was determined not to miss the fun and be disappointed. He had gone anyway.

When a blizzard blew up in the small hours it wasn't very pleasant out there, especially for my friend who was literally caught with his trousers down a time or two.

Like I said, sea anglers have to be tough. Exposure wasn't the word for it!

11

Darkie Charlie and Saltwater Trout

THE average angler's knowledge of the fish he tries to catch is akin to the general level of understanding the motorist has about what goes on under the bonnet. The vast majority of drivers are only really willing to show an interest when something is wrong and the same can be said of fishermen, for as long as fish are there for the taking they are not too bothered about the health of the fish themselves.

Mind you, we are in a rather different position. The driver does have instruction books and manuals to turn to if he wants to know, whereas until relatively recently, it was not easy for the angler to know just where to turn if he was one of those who tried to find out more about his quarry.

Much of what we know has only been discovered or made readily available lately. Even now, it is probable that most fly fishermen, for example, know more about the life cycles of various insects they copy for their fly patterns than they do about the fish they are intending to catch.

There is a rudimentary understanding of what goes on in trout hatcheries, from the collection of the eggs, the fertilisation by milking the cock fish, and the tending of the fry through to the growing on in stew ponds. How short a time it is though since we learned of the genetic breakthrough that has led to the super trout. Men like Sam Holland, who turned a mind that helped in research that led to a man standing on the moon to ways of bringing fish farming up to date, have seen huge fish that were previously unimaginable become almost commonplace.

Of course, the monks of the Middle Ages knew about

rearing carp and, while we have forgotten much of what they practised, the east Europeans have advanced their production techniques. That is due, however, to the fact that carp are a delicacy in Poland and Czechoslovakia. Angling has had little to do with it, but the knowledge is being used for our benefit nonetheless.

Will freshwater fish, especially the carp, also become a recognised item on the British menu? With the price of sea fish going up alarmingly, there are those who believe it will. One of those who will be ready to meet such a demand is Roy Marlow who has put into practice everything he has been able to learn to make the Mallory Park Fisheries, not far from his Leicester tackle shop, one of the most prolific in the country.

His collaboration with the conservation element in his county has also led to the provision of a fifth lake in the race circuit complex. If – or perhaps, when – the housewife here decides the carp is good food and worth buying, Roy will be among the first to be able to supply her need. In the meantime, the lucky anglers at Mallory are the beneficiaries of his studies.

Compared with most of our coarse fisheries, which are left largely to restock themselves with little assistance from man, the sheer bulk of thriving fish in these shallow lakes is little short of amazing. I enjoyed one day there when my float was not given time to settle properly all day, such was the press of fish after my bait. Yet 13,000 bream had been netted from the same water only the week before!

But while much of the research going on into what really happens under the surface is being conducted with the provision of food for the world very much to the fore, the angler can reap rich rewards from the findings. The aim of much of the work going on is not so much to make fish grow bigger, but to enable them to reach a marketable size faster. This means that they are available at the right size – and the right price – sooner. But it does have the benefit, as far as the angler is concerned, of giving fish like the rainbow trout the chance to become much, much heavier during its allotted lifespan.

One advanced biological establishment I was fortunate to visit for a layman's glimpse of intriguing experiments was the

Fisheries Research Laboratory at Lowestoft. The fact that it is operated by the Ministry of Agriculture, Fisheries and Food, says it all as to what the scientists there are being paid to accomplish. But so many facets of their work have a bearing on angling it is just plain fascinating.

It was there I first heard of Darkie Charlie. He is a smaller member of the shark family who, like all sorts of other little-heard-of species of marine life, lives in the deep waters of the Atlantic off the Continental Shelf. Huge stocks of fish exist there, but they don't end up on the fishmonger's slab for two main reasons.

One is that it is much more difficult and costly to catch fish at these vast depths; the other – which really puts a brake on the development of effective techniques – is that if it isn't cod or plaice then the British housewife doesn't want to know about it.

How these fish thrive in such huge concentrations at those depths is incredible to anyone with no more than the sea angler's knowledge of saltwater. The pressure down there is such that the iron weights normally used to control the nets specially prepared to work in such water, were smashed – solid iron simply crushed! The only way to operate the equipment is to use solid rubber weights which change size as they are compressed into denser and denser balls without imploding.

And yet fish live out their lives down there.

It is fortunate that many of the biologists working there are anglers and continue to be involved with fish when they have time off. Needless to say, they know how to provide cod from the North Sea and trout from Ardleigh when fish are required for experimental purposes. And they also see the relevance to us of much of what is being learned in the continually unfolding pattern of marine existence.

They also know what is likely to make the ordinary angler's eyes open wide.

'Come and have a look in this tank. I think you'll be interested,' one of them told me. The 'tank' was a large concrete pond with a covered top that could be removed to open it up a section at a time. He pulled back one of the covers and popped in a handful of fish scraps. Immediately, the water 'boiled' as it does in any stock pond when trout are used to coming up to the splash for their goodies.

These were beautiful brown trout – deep-bodied, fast and fighting fit – weighing 2lb-plus, I estimated.

Then this much bigger, slower shape loomed up underneath before rising gently to the surface to swallow a morsel.

'What the hell was that?' I asked the laughing scientist. He had got the reaction he always expected.

'It's a turbot,' he said. There was a pause while I grasped what I was seeing.

'But they live in saltwater,' I said, dipping my finger into the tank and tasting it.

'That's right,' he said. 'This is saltwater.'

And he went on to explain what they were doing. Sea trout are only brownies that have decided to migrate, he explained, so it is obvious that brown trout can survive in saltwater. And, as sea trout tend to grow bigger, it seems logical to expect that they grow faster in the sea than they do in rivers.

The upshot of this reasoning was that they had taken some normally-reared brown trout and, over a period of about a fortnight, gradually changed the water in their tank from fresh to salt. Then, of course, they could happily join the turbot in their larger container.

The real advantage in fish-rearing terms soon became apparent. The brownies in brine were fed on fish offal which was much cheaper – around half the price – than the trout pellets their freshwater brethren were having to be fed. And on the fish diet they were growing at roughly twice the pace.

So a 1lb brownie raised by the normal methods could become a two-pounder in the same time span – and for far less outlay.

'All you have to do before you stock them in a river or reservoir is spend another couple of weeks removing the salinity from the water until they are living happily in freshwater again,' it was pointed out.

And once such fish are back in their expected surroundings, they revert naturally to the diet their smaller relatives have been on all the time.

Another interesting insight is that with the modern under-standing of fish genetics, it is possible to breed neuter fish that will not have the urge to attempt to spawn. In the case of the rainbow trout, this means that they will be fighting fit and good to eat all year long. This removes the problem of black cock fish early in the normal season when they can be an inedible nuisance. It also provides the opportunity, of which some fisheries have already taken advantage, to remain open and have fit fish for the catching all year round.

An interesting fact to emerge too, was that the same could be done with the turbot which grow at a rapid rate when cared for as at those Lowestoft premises. Naturally to rear fish for release into the open sea would be an impossibly small drop in the ocean, quite literally. But the prospect of an enclosed piece of sea water being stocked is perfectly feasible.

A put-and-take fishery that held 6 or 7lb turbot would appeal to a lot of saltwater anglers, I'm sure.

It was also enlightening to see the computations as regards nature's own way of restoring her plenty, given half a chance. While there is genuine concern for the fish population in the North Sea and its continued over-fishing, did you know that if, by some miracle, all the cod were to survive from a couple of years' spawnings, it would be possible to walk to Germany on them, so vast would be the sheer volume that would result?

Of course, that could not happen. But it is good to know that – mathematically, at least – if we clean up our act and give her a chance, nature will make sure that there are fish there for us to catch.

It was at the Lowestoft laboratory, too, that I talked with one of the team who had visited the Soviet Union to study their efforts to conserve the huge sturgeon in the Volga which are the source of that valuable commodity, caviare. He had been most impressed by what had been done to keep the route open to the spawning grounds when they migrate up the river each year. When a massive dam had been built as part of a hydro-electric scheme, a fish ladder was made impossible by the sheer size and height of the structure – and by the size of the fish.

So a lift had been constructed for them. Water flowing out of the open end of a tank at the bottom attracted the sturgeon inside. Once there, the end was sealed and they were raised to the top of the dam where they were allowed out through the other end into the lake that had been created.

It's no wonder that caviare is so expensive.

12

'Second-hand' Pleasure

THE way the foam was flying and the rod was bending made it plain this was no run-of-the-mill jack that had just taken the bait.

Discovering she was not as all-powerful as she had come to think, the huge pike surged off through the lilies, the taut line severing some, while the thrashing as she surfaced abruptly was rearranging others.

'Don't try and bully this one straight in,' I called, for it was my son who was holding the rod. Every pike he had caught until now he had been able to lock down on and take charge of. This one was different and, having tightened and struck fairly close in, he was reluctant to yield any of his 10lb line, especially with those lilies so handy. The high note of the singing nylon gave warning of a break not being far away.

There was no need to worry, however. He played it like a veteran, steering her into the restricted space between the weed beds, letting her calm down after that first flurry, then drawing her towards the large net held in my trembling hands when she tired.

That fight took far more out of me than if I had caught the fish myself – and certainly gave me more pleasure as well.

Knowing there were bigger fish there in addition to as near a guarantee of sport with smaller ones as you could find, I had taken him and my cousin's son piking. My role was purely to provide them with enough livebait.

A couple of smaller pike had made it a pleasant and worthwhile day by the time the sun sank behind the bank and the vapour rose as though kettles were boiling between the dew-soaked banks all along the river. It was then the float alongside the lilies plopped and line trickled from the spool to herald the real excitement of the trip.

That beautifully conditioned fish we lay in the grass weighed 22½lb, just that bit bigger than the best his father had ever landed to make it really memorable for the lad. It was obvious he would love to take it home and show family and friends. 'I know somebody who wants a big one to set up in a case for his hall,' he said. 'Shall we keep it?'

'You beat it,' I told him. 'It's your fish.'

'What would you do?'

'Well, if you put her back she will breed more big pike next spring and, who knows, she might make 30lb by the next time you or somebody else catches her again.'

He picked her up with difficulty, knelt by the water and gently put her back in her own element. For a moment she lay motionless before giving a sudden thrash of that spade of a tail that both startled and splashed all three of us. The spell was broken and we laughed excitedly.

The catch was relived several times during the walk through the cattle along the bank and the drive home. In the inevitable pause that followed all the chatter, he said, 'I'm glad I put her back. Seeing her shoot off like that was almost as good a feeling as catching her.'

We had another generation of anglers in the family.

Of course, things don't always work out as well as that, like the birthday 'treat' when a violent thunderstorm broke over Ringstead Grange and left us dumping handfuls of hailstones over the side of the boat. Well, it was July in England after all.

'Next time you have a clever idea, keep quiet about it and come on your own,' was the ungracious but understandable comment from the recipient of the 'gift'.

The days when he and other youngsters have enjoyed their fishing has given me huge satisfaction over the years though, the 'second-hand' pleasure often being every bit as enduring as the purely personal pride that can come from the attainment of a fishing goal. Many an angler has made that discovery which is why a boy interested in catching fish does not often have to look far for advice and encouragement. There are lots of 'Uncle Charlies' about.

I used to think most tackle dealers were as keen as most to get the kids involved; after all, it has to be good for business to put those who are potential customers for another fifty years on the right track. Now I'm not so sure. What made me wonder was the result of what I felt was one of the better ideas I had during my editorship of the trade's magazine. It was to put youngsters who wanted to improve their fishing in touch with the right people to help them. The editor of *Angling Times* agreed to carry a list of all tackle shops who would give the boys a welcome and either help them themselves or put newcomers in contact with competent fishermen among their customers who would show them the ropes.

My faith in the trade took a knock when only six shops throughout the entire country bothered to return the coupon we put in the magazine – and two of these I had talked into it myself. What a missed opportunity to put themselves on the side of the angels . . . and get some free advertising.

The National Anglers' Council have produced lots of qualified instructors through their training courses and many of them are showing beginners the right way. The Angling Foundation's 'Take a Friend Fishing' campaign is another major step towards making sure the sport does not become lost amid the competition with all the other things on offer for young people to do today – many of them much less palatable.

I heard of one young tearaway whose life was turned around thanks to a fishing rod – not used across his buttocks but placed in his hands. His escapades had gone beyond the prank stage before he was lucky enough to come across a member of the probation service who was trying fishing as therapy.

Getting him off concrete and on to the river bank literally opened his eyes to a whole new world. Anglers are great ones for accumulating sentimental 'treasures' and he soon found that he, too, had possessions to cherish in a way that had nothing to do with their cost. He really wanted to learn about something for the first time in his life; he began reading anything and everything about catching fish; his attitude towards school altered. He had found a purpose.

What a pity more of a generation, many of whom are

offered little in the way of hope, have not been given the same chance to expand their minds and their lives. Perhaps if more people were prepared to put the needs of these future citizens ahead of their desire for stagnation in the countryside, realising that in the process they would be turning them into the best of all conservationists, we could find out just what the true value of angling is.

Of course, our sport does suffer from one big obstacle as far as the beginner is concerned with which most other pastimes do not have to contend . . . the rod licence.

If someone wants to introduce a friend to his hobby, be it squash, tennis or horse-riding, golf, ping-pong or welly-wanging, he simply takes them along. There are clubs and associations that can be joined, if they feel so inclined once they have found out if they like it.

We're different. Stick a rod into someone's hand who shows an interest in angling and, unless you have gone through the performance of purchasing a rod licence, which gets dearer each year, you are creating an offence which could land them in court.

It isn't likely that any bailiff other than a complete idiot would prosecute in such circumstances, but a lot of dutiful and honest citizens don't like putting themselves or their children in a position where they could be summoned. And we still have all the other dues and demands common to other activities. It is in only few places that any right to actually fish is conferred with the licence. We still have to pay for the amenities we use like the followers of other duty-free sports. They receive grants; we pay an unwarranted tax.

Even some of the water authorities realise what a hindrance the licence is, for they have introduced free 'starter' licences for newcomers in their areas. But that piece of paper is still required.

The antiquated rod licence concept should have been swept away completely years ago. It is so costly to administer that much more of the anglers' money would be available to 'develop, maintain and improve fisheries' as the authorities are charged to do, if it were collected by any one of a dozen more

91

efficient means. The most sensible would be to add money to provide revenue for fishery management to the rents clubs already pay – a fishery levy (sounds better than rate or tax).

This would mean that the better, more popular and more expensive fisheries would have to pay more. And as it is more than likely that more people would want to fish improved waters, it would give an incentive for the spenders of the money to be wise with it as well.

Low rents would mean a poorer return. Look after the facilities and the waters would show a handsome return.

At present, the tackle dealer has to stop and sell licences at the busiest times of his year and for the smallest profit margin on any item he handles. And how preposterous it is that much of the money received for licences is spent on paying bailiffs just to make sure that the angler has one.

After all, why should anyone have to have a licence to carry a fishing rod?

Angling would do itself a very big favour if it were to campaign to get rid of this obstacle to anyone wanting to join us. The fraternity accept rod licences in the same way that they realise they are liable to get bitten by gnats. I suspect, however, that many newcomers who would rather not become involved with another piece of bureaucratic bumbledom go off and buy a pair of roller skates instead.

Without this sort of interference more people might discover that those who fish are less likely to suffer from mental illness or have a heart attack. In this health-conscious age, surely that is news worth turning into propaganda.

Mind you, there is always an exception to prove any rule, like the angler who failed to return home and was found dead on the bank still clutching a rod to which a hefty salmon had remained connected. I don't know whether the fish was released but it should have been, for it created a situation that gave a whole new meaning to the phrase 'Gone Fishin' '.

Whatever the advantages for themselves, some anglers are inclined not to enjoy the supplementary pleasure that can come from helping others join him by the water because they suffer from a feeling that the more people who go, the worse his own fishing will become. Indeed, the angler has always worried about increased pressure on the water available.

> If I, that am an angler, may protest,
>> Fishing is sweet pleasure, of sport the best,
> Of exercises the most excellent,
>> Of recreation the most innocent;
> But now the sport is marred, and wot ye why?
>> Fishes decrease – for Fishers multiply.

And that was written in 1598!

There is a great benefit from the added political pressure we can wield which comes from having more people aware of what fishing is all about. But there is more to it than that. For with fresh blood, there is more chance of those who are already committed discovering the pleasure to be found in helping someone else come to know that there is more to angling than dangling a handline from a harbour wall.

13

Two Records in a Day

GIVEN the huge army of anglers and the infinitely tiny percentage who can have their name inscribed on the record roll of honour, it is perhaps not surprising that the vast majority have never even glimpsed a record fish.

While we all half-hope that we might just capture such a monster one day, most of us are well aware that we are not likely to see it happen.

It is pretty certain that more people saw Dick Walker's record carp than have seen all the other records put together. That venerable old lady was admired by many thousands of people. During her years in the acquarium at London Zoo, Clarissa or Ravioli, as she was also known, probably had nearly as big a part to play in the growth of carp angling as did her captor.

There was a memorable day, however, when I very nearly encountered two record fish of different species – and one of them a record roach at that!

It was back in the sixties when, though the four-minute-mile barrier had been broken, there was still doubt over whether roach grew to be bigger than 4lb or not. Dennis Landamore of Norwich believed they did when he caught a fish well over that weight in a 40lb bag of roach from a shallow swim on the River Yare five miles above the city.

When he took a scale as big as a fivepence piece and put it on the counter in Ken Smith's shop, the tackle dealer also thought Dennis must have made history.

'It was too colourful for a bream and yet, if it were from a roach, it must be a record breaker,' Ken said.

The fish was fetched and, when weighed on the accurate scales in the greengrocer's next door, it registered 4lb 6oz. It revived in Ken's livebait tank but the more they looked at it, the more they convinced themselves it had to be a roach/bream hybrid. It was a busy Saturday, however, and so the fish stayed there over the weekend until Ken could get down to some serious scale and fin counting on the Monday.

The fish looked the part, although there was a slight 'breamy' hump to the back. But the red fins and the touch of gilt had one or two experienced big fish men declaring that it had to be a roach.

Mathematically, it was 17 inches long and 6 inches deep. It had 46 scales along the lateral line (bream have 49–57 and roach 40–50); the anal fin had 16 branched rays (bream have 26 to 31 and roach 9 to 12) there were just one too many rays in the dorsal fin as well; and there were 5½ rows of scales between the lateral line and the pelvic fins whereas there should have been four.

By now the detective work was getting too technical and nobody was prepared to say it was a roach – or that it wasn't!

So Peter Tombleson, secretary of the British Record (rod-caught) Fish Committee, was notified and came over from Peterborough in the afternoon.

He felt it must be a hybrid. But he was not willing to commit himself totally either. His further examination of the scales revealed the fish to be 11 years old whereas a roach of 3lb-plus is usually 14 or 15. Of course, however, it could have enjoyed a rich diet.

The scales also showed that the fish had not spawned. This again, was not conclusive but it did not help the potential claim for, though hybrids do breed, it is more likely for them to be sterile than a true roach.

In the end, the fish had to be placed in formalin and sent on to Liverpool University where its backbone was X-rayed and its teeth examined to make certain. The diagnosis was that it was a hybrid which was about 80 per cent roach, probably with a bream in its family a generation or two back.

Ten years before, that fish would have become the new roach record. As Peter Tombleson said, no one would have had the facilities to be able to say it was not one without the newly introduced methods of examining fish when checking record claims.

'At least,' he told a disconsolate Dennis, 'when someone does catch a 4lb roach we know just what it will look like.'

While all the checks on the 'roach' were going on, the second 'record' was brought into Ken's shop. Swimming happily in a bucket was 'a ruffe that weighed 5oz when it was caught yesterday'.

Captor was Brian Curtis of Sprowston who had taken it during an Oddfellows Angling Club match on the River Ant. The club scales were not designed for measuring such minute species in detail, however, so Peter Tombleson took that back to Peterborough as well for verification on the Record Committee's equipment which was accurate to within ½ dram.

There was no doubt about the identification of the species as far as this spikey little monster was concerned and, with the ruffe record then standing at 3oz 9dr, there was more optimism about this fish's record potential.

It was shown, however, to weigh exactly 3oz 6dr, which would have equalled the previous best. So the Norwich driving instructor's mini-goliath did not make it into the record books.

All the excitement left us with nothing but a good story. Two records were intact.

Now there are those anglers who argue that the record list is not really important. It is just a matter of being in the right place at the right time and being particularly lucky, they claim. They could be right, but there are those who dedicate their lives to being the man to land the biggest that has ever been known. Even the sceptics have to admit, if they're honest, that being the captor of the biggest carp, bass, pike or cod would be rather nice.

Where it does get a bit silly is with regard to some of those smaller specimens. Like that ruffe, for example. I don't know anybody who has ever deliberately set out to catch one of those little horrors (except in desperate match situations, that is). Bream anglers hate to see them in the swim, for once they move on to your bait, the bream clear off . . . they don't like them either.

And did you know that, in less enlightened times, the ruffe was also called the Pope. As a mark of celebrating their religious freedom, people in some places used to push corks on to those prickly dorsal fins on some former saints' days and watch the fish suffer. Lots of fishermen don't love the cocky ruffe any better today.

The question is, does anybody really desire to have his name listed as being the 'sportsman' to have conquered the biggest one of them?

On the sea front, it has really become something of a joke though. Lots of little sea fish are on the record list, some of which are of a kind nobody but crossword compilers in difficulties have ever heard of otherwise.

Take the three-bearded rockling for instance. A spate of captures of veritable monsters of their kind several summers ago led to claims for a succession of records – mostly concerning fish in the 3 to 3½oz category and landed on 20lb line and cod hooks.

I was on *Angling Times* at the time and one reporter pretty well got himself elected as the three-bearded rockling specialist, with everyone else promptly passing any reference to them over to him.

By coincidence, the first telephone answering machine arrived in the office at the same time. It meant that anyone ringing up with information at any time of day or night would hear a friendly voice and that their story would be followed up as soon as someone came in.

Of course, a message had to be recorded on the tape to greet the readers who would make use of the service.

'Thank you for ringing us,' it said. 'We're sorry the office is unattended at the moment but if you would like to leave your name and number we'll contact you as soon as possible.'

There were, however, a few seconds left and the long-suffering rockling reporter who was taping the message just could not resist ad libbing 'But if it's about a three-bearded rockling, stick it up . . .' You can imagine the rest.

The trouble was that when the staff had finished laughing at the joke, it was discovered that no one knew how to wipe the tape clean and re-record the text without the addition.

It was nearly a fortnight before a representative called to erase the offending passage so that we dared to leave the new machine switched on.

On reflection, I believe so many anglers share my feelings about some of these lists of tiny fish nobody actually tries to catch, that it was perhaps a pity we didn't leave that heart-felt comment for the world to hear.

14
Learning from the Experts

IT has always surprised me how people can change in stature when they're doing something they are really good at. Like great footballers who appear totally different from the dominant figures out there on the pitch when they're sitting and talking afterwards. Or the actor who seems an ordinary sort of guy until he gets on a stage and the spotlight hits him; then he takes on a whole new dimension.

The same can be said of many top anglers I've met. They don't necessarily stand out in the crowd, but when they are on the bank, in that element in which they can express themselves, they certainly don't merge into the background.

Instinctively the rest of us know this, which is part of the reason you can be sure where they are at important matches. For, if there are any spectators around, they automatically congregate to form a gallery behind these men with charisma whether they are catching on the day or not.

Of course, there are exceptions. Peter Anderson, for instance, whose presence in his kilt makes sure you can't overlook him anywhere. But even he took on that larger-than-life aura when delighting thousands at the Boat Show or the Game Fair with his fly-casting performances. And though big Kevin Ashurst is never likely to be lost in the crowd, he too is the more remarkable when he is controlling that float through the rod as though the tackle were all an extension of his arm.

It is not just these top exponents who can catch the eye, though, for there is an inherent curiosity in all of us that makes us want to know what someone else is doing, particularly if he is obviously good at it. Every fisherman is aware of this fact because, if there are people around, he is sure to be looked at and questioned. If there is a picnic area near the reservoir bank from which he is fishing, he will have to be careful not to hook those creeping up behind him who get a bit too nosey; if he is on a towpath, a few fish can mean a group of Sunday morning strollers watching him anywhere.

The odd thing is though that many people who fish themselves take little advantage of the chance to improve which is offered by observing these top men in the sport. Every aspiring batsman studies the cricket experts, seeks coaching and looks to his technique, yet men who hope to cast a sea lead twice as far as even Botham can bash a ball, often have little time left after their own fishing trips to take a look at the masters.

Among fly fishermen, some do search out the experts who can put them right, but the vast majority of coarse anglers as well as many sea and fly men have never had any kind of tuition or instruction nor spent more than the odd minute looking at the experts.

Perhaps it is because they don't like to admit there is anyone that much better than themselves from whom they could learn. I have felt for years that the tackle trade lives on ego. When the average angler accepts that he is beaten by the 'crack' at the next peg because the man is a better angler, it will be a sad day for the industry. It is always due to the draw, the line he's using, his rod, his reel, his bait . . . there are always dozens of things to explain any failure; it's a wonderful sport for excuses. Seldom does Mr Average have to admit it's his own fault and that he has not done his homework, has not practised and does not know the venue.

Consider the average local club who have decided to enter a team in the national championships. They read up about the water which is new to them and on which they are going to have to compete . . . and that is mostly match results. They ask advice (usually suspect) from the odd person they know who has fished there on holiday. One or two of the dozen actually make the effort to go there to fish it.

Sometimes, in what they see as a bid to really examine the venue, they organise an outing or two to fish the water in advance. This inevitably takes the form of a match, often part of the season's fixture list which goes towards an over-all trophy. Everybody is fishing for himself as he would anywhere else; little information is shared until afterwards when it is too late to put anything learned into practice or carry out any worthwhile experiment.

When they fail miserably on the day, unless one or two of them get lucky, they come up with a variety of reasons and carry on just the same next year.

What they ought to do, of course, is look for a big match on that water not too long before their event. Then they can go and watch the local aces and the visiting 'names', sacrificing their own fishing purely to go and learn. It might feel like a wasted day's fishing, but it would do them more good than all the matches they can fit in when they only fish among themselves and don't employ that 'Curiosity Factor'.

There are few sports where you can get so close to the men who can really demonstrate the short-cuts to success, but most fishermen never take the chance that is there. I was lucky in that it was a part of my job to have to attend some of the top events, matches where only those who had learned their craft thoroughly were going to be taking part. Studying these 'professionals' was a route that saved hours of trial and error. They had done it all already.

Events to look for are those like the Division I National where you won't get many anglers in the teams who don't know what they are doing. With so many good outfits fishing today it is only the best who can get to this top level and stay there. Every section contains several anglers who, while not necessarily covering themselves with glory on the day, will show just how to make the most of the swims they have drawn.

Super League matches, open invitation events, the final rounds of inter-club knock-out contests . . . they are all going to bring a lot of excellent anglers together in one place. Spectators can learn a lot, and yet so few bother to go along.

With international matches taking place in the fly fishing world now, the same thing applies. Every major beach festival also brings superb casters and men who understand the sea together. Whatever sort of fishing you do, the experts are available for scrutiny.

The last World Coarse Angling Championships in the UK provided a chance many did take to see what the superstars could do. In spite of the weather, the associated mud and the route march from the car park, few who went would have been happy to miss it. The problem was that you really need feeding fish for even these men to show how they can charm them out of the water.

One superb occasion when far too few took advantage of the opportunity to see some experts 'on' fish, was the Sundridge festival weekend at Holme Pierrepont near Nottingham. In the afternoon, a French team opened several eyes as to the virtue of long pole tactics. The arrival of the method on the British scene probably dates from then and the mastery displayed by people like Guy Hebert.

The alternating anglers had to use their 'own' methods and Ian Heaps had to stick with the waggler, while his French neighbour ran an 11-metre pole back and forth on rollers while unshipping it to pop such a succession of small fish into his net that he doubled the former world champion's weight.

In the evening, however, it was a different story for the bream fed and John Dean was able to give a demonstration of long-range float fishing that paralysed the French contingent.

That float fishing maestro Robin Harris performed a similar feat on the Nene, which is virtually his backyard, in the memorable *Angling Times* 21st anniversary match between English and French teams. He gave a graceful and stylish example of British fishing which showed just why he is the only man ever to win a National and the World title. That day it was the continental method that did not suit the conditions.

Perhaps the greatest lesson to be learned by all those who have added a pole to their armoury and know how to make one work is when and when not to use it.

One man who learned that lesson probably sooner than anyone else on this side of the Channel was Ray Mumford who put on one of the most memorable match fishing displays I had the privilege of watching when he won the first Gladding Masters on the Nene. It was the London angler's controversial attitude and certainly not his ability that kept him out of the England squad.

Taking on the best matchmen of the seventies, including Kevin Ashurst, his dad Benny and local hero Robin Harris, Ray had done his homework, and as usual, was impeccably prepared. Knowing that Robin hates the millions of tiny bleak in the river and that most of the field would follow his lead and try for roach and bream, Ray went for these fifty or sixty to the pound mini-fish from the outset. After half an hour he had caught only a handful on his short rod – not the expected pole – and all the intelligentsia nodded; he had blown it.

But persistent feeding with very dry groundbait drew the bleak to him and for the next four and a half hours he kept up a rhythm that was a delight to watch, at several points raising his catch rate to six a minute. At the whistle he had 752 of the tiny fish to put on the scales for a clear cut winning weight of, I believe, about 14lb.

A subsequent Gladding was also won with small fish against all the odds. Lancashire's Alan Webber set his stall out for the tiny gudgeon when it was held on Walter Bower's stretch of the Trent. He conjured up a total of around 16lb of them, more than enough to take the title from a star-studded field who were after chub, roach and carp.

One of the men he beat that day is probably the most loved of all the aces as far as the gallery is concerned because he is also the most outgoing of the upper echelon – Ivan Marks. Whereas his former Leicester colleague Roy Marlow earned his reputation by arriving at decisions by systematically solving problems in a diligent, scientific way, Ivan is an intuitive angler.

Instinctively he knows the right thing to do. He does things which are right because they feel right to him and, like that other great England performer, former world champion Ian Heaps, he has a phenomenal memory.

Both of them can recall, almost fish for fish it seems, matches they fished years ago. This enables them to come up with answers to situations by pulling from the files of their minds the details of winning tactics – and then having the ability and versatility to make them work.

Ian, perhaps more than anyone, is taking the word to the

angler, for his road shows, run in conjunction with Ray Baker of DAM, fill halls all over the country each winter. It isn't quite the same as seeing him in action on the bank, but it gives anglers a chance to pick a top brain.

Another wonderful performance I was on hand to witness was given by Percy Anderson, the popular Cambridge match-winner, when he took his National title on the Welland. It was a dour match in conditions far from promising or pleasant on that open venue, and he was not in a favoured area either. In fact, at one stage it looked like being remembered only as the day when Jimmy Randell and Roy Marlow had to walk to their pegs for being late for the buses at the start.

But Percy changed all that. When the man a few pegs away caught one of the hoped-for bream, Percy laid a thick carpet of casters in his swim and waited for them to move. His know-ledge of the Fen waters served him well for though others around him all caught one or two from the shoal of hefty 'Humphreys', they eventually settled in front of him.

With the familiar cigar between his trembling lips, he con-centrated completely on the swingtip to make sure there would be no mistake that would scare them. Wearing a thin plastic folding raincoat, for he had not expected this sort of weather and had nothing warmer with him, his teeth chattered as the rain ran off the 'pixie' hood. He looked worn out and frozen as he finally lit his smoke at the whistle, but that masterly 42lb carved Percy his permanent niche in angling history.

Strangely perhaps, it is with regard to casting techniques rather than actual fishing that many seem prepared to look to their betters. There probably are not as many excuses here as when fish themselves are involved! Watching John Holden send 5oz of lead nearly a furlong when testing a rod being made for him, for instance, was a salutary experience for a mere 100-yard man. It is with the fly rod that the precision and the delicate timing which makes the expert can probably be demonstrated at its best – and more safely. Packed galleries watch enthralled at country fairs every summer as the men who have mastered the art take over from the majority having a try at the casting competitions.

Outstanding among the contestants was a young man who so impressed the knowledgeable gathering at one Game Fair that they have invited Alan Tonkin back to demonstrate ever since. How that kind of seemingly effortless casting towers above the rest of us was brought home on a Scottish holiday. Out in a boat on Coldingham Loch I pointed to two figures in another boat over 600 yards away.

Even at that distance I was able to tell my son, 'That's better casting than we have seen all week.' So we drifted over so that he could take a closer look. How right I was we discovered when we stopped for a chat with Ian Blagburn and John Gibson of Hardys who were up from Alnwick for the evening. And if you get a chance to see Jim Hardy using a fly rod, don't miss it, for he made a huge impression on the Japanese when he showed them how it should be done a few years ago.

Another noted caster who has delighted crowds and helped hundreds is Yorkshire's Jack Martin. How quickly he can help people came in a personal example when, in a matter of seconds, he sorted out my problem (well, one of them, anyway). 'Just put your right foot in front, not the left one,' was all he said when he saw me putting out a line. It is such a simple thing, but no one had told me before. It made me more accurate and stopped me rotating instead of letting the rod do its work. I've passed on the advice to dozens of trout men since with the same improvement following.

Another great man with a fly rod I was privileged to meet was the late Lionel Sweet. He was 75 when the Wizard of the Usk, who held the world salmon fly distance record for years, showed me he had retained his mastery with a fly rod near the bridge in his home town.

Not necessarily of fish, but of such occasions are an angler's memories measured.

The best advice for anyone aspiring to improve in any facet of the sport is to keep an eye open for when you will have the chance to see a man who has proved himself. You're bound to learn a lot and the odds are that he will be delighted to offer all the help he can. You might even find he's as impressive without a rod in his hand.

15

Working Parties

– and other things to do in the close season

A BUTCHER and a retired farmer scythed reeds while a schoolteacher sweated profusely as he strove to keep pace carrying the debris away with a pitchfork.

A bank manager was digging into a clay bank on the other side of the lake, liberally splashing the policeman companion he was helping build a footbridge over a dyke from old bricks and a pallet.

A lot of banging was coming from a landing stage where the treasurer, who tried to keep it quiet that he worked for the Inland Revenue, was clouting nails into new boards.

A huge bonfire was in grave danger of setting light to an entire plantation not far from where a doctor and a second teacher were slapping paint on to the old railway wagon affectionately known as the lodge, themselves and everything within about 6 feet.

Two technically-minded members – one a railway engine driver and the other a fitter with the gas board – were alternately hitting a mower with spanners and swearing at it.

And the chairman, who owned the local tackle shop, was making tea on a primus for the close-season-affected anglers who were spending their Sunday raising blisters on their hands.

It was the annual working party.

These occasions can be a lot of fun if they are approached in the right frame of mind. Firstly, you have to be prepared to do any dirty job going – and smile; secondly, it is essential to ignore the advice which is given by everybody who only half did it last year or the year before – which is why you're doing it again now; and thirdly, agree with the master plan, then get on and do what you like the same as the rest are doing.

What needs attending to and how it should be tackled is always agreed by the committee meeting in a nice warm room somewhere – probably in a pub – well in advance while the image in their minds is still of the water as it was last summer. By the time you get there, so much has changed that most of what was wanted is not wanted any more. The committee don't want to look silly, so they hide the blueprints and everybody gets stuck in where he feels like it.

And every year, by some minor miracle, the water is fine for opening day.

You often learn a lot that helps your fishing, too. For example, one spring we decided to clear a gap in a lily bed. A meat hook was bought from a firm specialising in supplying butchers and spliced to a length of '18-stone' Manilla rope. With five men doing a fair impression of a tug o' war team we eventually straightened that galvanised hook after getting it well and truly embedded in the roots. I've never felt too bad about losing a size 18 to a 1lb hook length in the lilies since.

Sometimes, of course, there are accidents. Like the time Doug was so pleased with the swim he had cleared and dug to provide armchair comfort that he stepped back to admire his handiwork – straight into 8 feet of cold water.

The happenings can also be much more spectacular and – with the help of hindsight – predictable. Take the bedstead, for instance.

We had cut away offending branches, chopped down nettle beds and generally made every available swim habitable. But there was an island that would give access to open water and, though it was small, there would be room for at least two to fish there very comfortably. 'If we had a raft, we could pop back and forth with our gear,' someone said.

It was at one of those nocturnal, indoor get-togethers that the idea really mushroomed and someone had the further inspiration of offering for use an old bedstead they wanted to get rid of. 'If we fit it up, wire it and nail it, we'll have a solid frame,' he pointed out. 'If we put a lot of 10-gallon drums underneath, it will take all the weight we need.'

Another helpful soul chimed in, 'I can get all the cans we want.' The raft construction team sorted itself out and from there on it just snowballed. The little boys buried in those relatively sensible men came to the surface the next Sunday morning when all the paraphernalia was assembled on the bank.

Perhaps, if the drums had been fixed under solid timber instead of being held only by the bed springs the raft would have been more stable, but though they did have a tendency to move around, it seemed safe enough.

I got on one end. Colin got on the other, and sent me 2 feet into the air. He weighed a lot more than I did. But he had wellies on so it didn't matter that his end was ankle deep in the lake. We balanced it as best we could and quanted gently away from the shore, had our pictures taken, then punted just as gently back again.

'I don't think you'll get a lot of tackle over there on that,' I said.

'Go on, that's safe enough. We'll just shove a few more drums under next time we're here,' they said.

'We haven't been to the island yet,' Cyril pointed out. It was only 30 feet away and it did seem a shame. It was decided that if the guy with the camera went he could picture the raft with all the workers in the background. I promptly let him have my place.

Now swans were nesting on the island and the cob didn't look too enthusiastic about all the commotion near his home. So it was decided three should go – one to stay aboard and a third man to go ashore to guard the photographer in case, when his back was turned, Father Swan decided to repel boarders.

Cyril joined the photographer and Colin and all went well on the outward and obviously overloaded journey. Complete with pole, he kept an eye on the swans as we were captured for posterity. The photographer re-embarked smoothly, but when Cyril – last man to leave – stepped down it was a bit further then he had thought.

The bedstead rocked. His two companions moved to counter the list and steady the craft . . . and rocked it alarmingly the other way. It was when all three, as one man, jumped back the other way to stabilise it that they turned it right over.

Cyril was catapulted into the air and seemed almost to bounce as he hit the surface, swimming so strongly that we never did find his wellies.

Like the Lady of the Lake, the photographer's arm sank gracefully beneath the waves, clutching the camera as he went. He said afterwards, 'There I was sitting on the bottom in 8 feet of water with the camera still held above my head thinking, "You fool, it's 4 feet down anyway and you'll drown if you just sit here".'

We never did fish from the island. The bedstead was hauled from the water, carried round to some overgrown woods at the back and dumped. As far as I know it's still there.

They really can be fun, these working parties.

Don't run away with the idea that preparing for a new season, whether for trout or coarse fish, is the only thing to do during the enforced closure. You can always be like some of those with whom I trout fish and have a 'standing order' one day a week on a charter boat from autumn until spring to keep the withdrawal symptoms from getting a hold.

Trouble is, it can be a bit expensive. So how about a bit of babbing during those lovely spring evenings when coarse anglers can't put a line on the water? Babbing is also known as bunching or totting in some parts of the country, and is the art of catching eels without a hook on the line.

A garden cane makes an ideal rod and stout cord is the line tied to the end of it. The real business is done by the bab, tot or bunch which is tied to the line. This is made up of wool which must be the worsted kind, modern nylon yarns definitely not doing the job as well.

With a baiting needle – a large darning needle will do – you thread lobworms on to the wool lengthways. The bigger they are, the better.

Getting enough lobs is another sport in its own right. You need a neatly clipped lawn which need not necessarily be your own, though if you use someone else's make sure they know so you don't get arrested. Not that trespassing in pursuit of worms would be much of a charge on which to come before the magistrates, but you do have to collect them in the dark, quietly and with a hooded light. And it all looks very sinister if a neighbour doesn't expect to see you creeping about in his garden during the hours of darkness.

If you stamp your feet, even walk carelessly, or flash the light about the worms will vanish. And they can move backwards down their holes faster than your mates can get their glasses on the bar when you say it's your round. Generations of blackbirds have trained them to do it.

You must tread stealthily with the shielded beam showing just the patch of grass you can reach from your bent position. When it picks out a lobworm on the surface with its tail in its hole, you have to grab it near the tail end, hold on as it contracts, then ease it from its sanctuary.

You will need about a yard of them to make a good bab, the length of wool-impregnated worms then being coiled up and tied to the end of your line.

Eels are sure to be found congregated below weir sills or other obstructions in a river at the time of year when they run up the water courses, and in the same spots when they move out to sea again in the autumn. They can be taken nearly anywhere on the right muggy night though. And they will follow the scent of your worm bunch from miles away, being even more likely to appear if a few of you are close together.

The way it works is that the eels bite into the bunch of worms and get their teeth caught in the wool. You just lift gently when you feel the unmistakable pull, for if you strike you'll knock them off. You swing the eel over a tub or bath and shake it off. A bucket isn't big enough for this receptacle but an old umbrella upside down is perfect.

Over-enthusiastic lifting can create a catapult effect and result in airborne eels and the need for a secondary group whose job is to hunt them in any adjacent grass and nettle beds. But if you know someone who likes eels you've got a good excuse for some real close season fun.

112

16

A Meeting of
Like Minds?

IT took only one glance at the agenda to know we were in for
a long night.

The scene was typical of many thousands of others; the
angling club was holding its annual meeting and the venue was
the 'Headquarters' – better known as the back room of the
chairman's local.

As at any similar gathering, the regulars who form the
committee that meets here once a month throughout the year,
greet one another and get the beer in. The 'ordinary' members
vary in number from none (everybody who turned up last year
was elected to the committee) to several hundred, the atten-
dance depending more on whether something important is due
for an airing than the numerical strength the particular
association is reputed to have.

The influx of seldom-seen subscription payers at our version
of the ritual, and the way in which they were collecting into
distinct groups, did not bode well for a 'rubber-stamping' of
the committee's recommendations. The agenda did not pin-
point the specific item of interest; there were several candi-
dates. Hence the suspicion that those who were laying in a
supply of refreshment to prevent their vocal chords drying out
were being wise.

As it was a coarse club, the most likely reason for the
upsurge in numbers at the meeting was Item 6: 'Increase in
subs.' Most coarse fishermen believe deep down that their
sport should really cost them nothing, so any hint at the annual
toll for their pleasure being raised from, say, £3 to £3.50 is
liable to lead to a minor rebellion among the ranks and calls

for the treasurer's head on a platter.

Perhaps Item 9: 'Continued membership of the NFA' had something to do with the better-than-average turn-out, for that would be linked to the issue of how much was having to be paid for the direct affiliation to the hierarchy.

Item 11 looked a likely suspect as well: 'Proposed ban on pike and eels from match weights'. Maybe it was actually something related to fishing that had drawn these men from their warm firesides on this blustery winter night. For it is a strange but little-known fact that anglers who will stick it out for five hours in the worst that nature can conjure up for them after travelling long distances on frozen roads, are unable to attend meetings a quarter of a mile away in winds above Force 3 or when it is drizzling.

The hardy annual of into which winter league, or leagues (if any) a team, or teams, should be entered was also on the list of interest rousers. And there was a suggestion that there should be more outings to different waters. 'Juvenile matches' and 'Annual dinner' were not likely to be the attraction any more than the election of officers or the presentation of the balance sheet – just so long as it showed some sort of a profit.

As it turned out, several people wanted to voice their opinions on many of the matters.

Some of the comments were sound and won wide support, like 'The rules stop us fishing for pike in matches so it seems silly that they should be included' and 'If we don't weigh eels we'll have nothing to put on the scales sometimes' during the debate on the proposed bans.

In the end, pike were removed from the match weight reckoning. And to show fate has a sense of humour, the mover of the proposition landed one of 3½lb in the first match the next season that would have won him a cup if it could have been counted. But we didn't know that when his eloquence won approval.

Other arguments made you wonder which planet the speculators spent their time on. Who, for instance, could expect to sell a single ticket to an annual dinner if it were held on 16 June? But that is what somebody seriously suggested before being howled down from all sides.

More disturbing was the consideration some were prepared to give to a proposition that all support be withdrawn from junior matches until the miser, who saw it as a means of saving a few pence on his subscription without realising it could bring about the long-term end of the club, was shamed into a retraction.

A 'five-minute recess' at 10 o'clock to replenish the glasses but which lasted twenty did not help to shorten the occasion. The manner in which the agenda was ignored and altered to suit the mood, as well as how propositions were accepted, helped protract matters, too.

For instance, when someone proposed an extra £1 on the subscriptions, another member suggested £1.50 would be preferable, and a third called for them to remain as they were. There was pandemonium when the chairman simply called for a ballot by saying, 'Right, all those in favour raise your hands.' Everyone thought he was voting for his own particular cause as the arms went up and all three looked like being 'carried unanimous' until the ensuing unscrambling straightened out the issue; three separate votes being required to leave things just as they were.

The meeting eventually ground to a close with about half those listed as attending still present, some time after midnight.

And there was a message here for anyone having a cause to plead at any meeting anywhere – make it obvious you're prepared to settle in for a long debate during 'any other business' at that time of night and you can find all sorts of support from people who'll vote for anything just so long as they can go home soon.

As one of the stalwarts commented pointedly though, 'If we can sit on a bank for five hours every week, it won't hurt us to spend as long getting things straight once a year.'

It is clear that not many agree, however, and the over-riding problem with angling politics is that an important part of going fishing is to get away from the hassle created by 'political' problems of one sort or another which people have to face

115

in their lives every day.

Most fishermen opt out of any administrative involvement by claiming that they want to relax through their sport, not become caught up in another series of headaches.

While most of them will talk for hours about fish and matters related to them, however remotely, they don't want the onus of doing the work that comes with making the fishing available to fall on them. It is understandable, of course, but it is one of the major factors that makes us so vulnerable when the sport comes under attack.

When what became known as the 'Swans and Lead' issue first blew up, the most commonly expressed view was that we were just too big for officialdom to dare do anything silly like interfere with our affairs, and that included what weights we used. Those thousands who had never seen a dead swan on the bank, or only the odd one which had taken off into a power line, could not accept the suspect figures purported to reflect our culpability in the demise of a species later shown to be increasing in numbers in any case.

They stocked up with lead weights in case there was a ban – and ignored the matter.

Now we know we are not inviolate.

There is, thank goodness, a nucleus who like being angling's leaders and who will take the initiative in any such fight. The very nature of the pastime, however, seems to mean that they have few followers who will join the fray, unless they are personally affected by the case in hand. Why else would the Anglers' Co-operative Association receive such derisory support?

Without doubt, not only the biggest safeguard that angling has in its stance against pollution at all levels, they are one of the most effective conservation bodies in any sphere in the UK. Yet the scant backing they get from the angling public leaves them walking a financial tightrope. As I've said before, if only all the rod licence revenue went to them instead of largely disappearing into the monetary morass of the water authorities, what a safe world it would be for those who delight in being able to sally forth with a rod in their hand.

Don't believe for a moment, however, that the coarse angler is the only one to avoid his administrative responsibilities wherever possible. Sea anglers don't often surface until some-one threatens to close the local pier to them. And there are some wonderful 'status quo' merchants among the fly fishing ranks. No, not heavy metal rock fans, but Luddites who would destroy the very mechanics of change.

A couple of fine examples came from a small fishery that always seems to have a large residue of trout which have not been accounted for by the end of the season.

Perhaps – it was suggested by one of the regulars – an 'Any method' weekend to round off the season would be a good idea. Selling however many fish we could catch would give us an additional amount to spend on stocking for the coming year – over-wintering in cash rather than in kind, as one person put it.

After all, it was argued, there was a fair head of pike in the lake and it was certain they did not stop taking trout when we did. After six months of steady feeding, they must be making sizeable inroads into the uncaught fish present in October. With natural losses in bad weather, the percentage of trout surviving to rise to a fly in the spring had to be pretty small.

It didn't take long for the dyed-in-the-wool brigade to cry 'Maggot Murderers' and 'Coarse Cretins'. When one used the word 'Sacrilege' it gave a pointed indication as to the feeling such arguments can evoke; there was something bordering on religious belief involved in some of the thinking.

When the suggestion was thrown out without a decent hearing, on emotional rather than logical grounds, in order to avoid the taint some saw we would be bringing upon ourselves by taking trout with anything other than a fly, a further matter was raised.

It was pointed out that each year the catch returns from the water produced a graph remarkably like an enlarged picture of the edge of a saw blade. Soon after the fish went in, a point of one of the teeth cropped up. This went down in a gradual curve which trickled on at a low level until the steep climb to another point marked the next stocking.

Now, if there were more stockings, it was reasoned, while the peaks would obviously not be as high, that decline before the next high point would not be as prolonged either. The residue at the end of the year would be reduced and the picture would be heading towards the ideal catch return situation – a straight line with fishing potential good all season.

At present there were four stockings and it was countered that if there were more regular visits from the fish farm, the fishery would soon be spending more on transport than would be left to pay for the fish which would, therefore, be fewer in number. It was discovered, however, that the fish farm owner was prepared to make more drops for the syndicate for the same money, if they were prepared to fit in with deliveries to other waters which took him their way.

The commonsense suggestion was to have as many stockings as he was willing to make – the same number of fish being split into deliveries as frequent as he was able to provide for the same outlay.

The majority of the syndicate members, however, steadfastly refused to consider any more than their four stockings. They even blocked any suggestion that the matter be discussed further with the fish supplier.

Beat that for obstinate adherence to a policy that precluded any possibility of improvement.

Yet those self-same people paid regular visits – and 'paid' was the operative word – to other waters where they knew the odds were more heavily in their favour due entirely to the put-and-take stocking, sometimes on even a daily basis.

As far as I know, up to a quarter of the trout expensively purchased and stocked there are still 'unaccounted' for each season.

I do not believe this is an isolated case either.

One water authority did some research to try and solve this riddle of uncaught fish by marking trout stockings in a small gravel pit; the problem was that noticeable. They found that the rainbows were mostly caught within a couple of weeks of going in. After that, they became almost uncatchable.

That was until the next batch was put in. Their colour

coding system showed that each stocking not only provided the expected new fish to catch, but the residents came on the feed and turned up in the bags again as well.

All the unscientific and purely personal observation that I and several friends have culled from long assocation with waters around the country, would tend to bear out this conclusion entirely.

So how many small fisheries are missing out by not putting their fish into the water as thinly as possible? The ones who suffer worst, of course, are those with a policy of just one in-put at the start of the season – and a steady decline in the catch-rate throughout the year.

Apart from all the other problems they have, it's difficult for these anglers to fish with their fingers crossed from somewhere around July onwards!

And a lot of it is down to the fact that the meetings at which such decisions are taken are not as well attended as they might be. Most anglers – whether in a club, an association or a syndicate – have one chance a year to try and put things right. Most of them don't take it; they grumble about the fishing instead.

17

Why are they laughing at us?

THE person who has spent any length of time trying to do it knows that to be a successful catcher of fish requires patience, dedication and total concentration. And that makes it a serious business.

So why is it that to the uninitiated, we create such an ideal figure at which fun can be poked; a butt for jokes; a target for ridicule?

The fool at one end with a worm on the other is an oft-quoted description of us which is happily accepted, even by those whose spare time is devoted to nothing better than knocking a little white ball into a distant hole in the ground. After all, they could always make the hole bigger and stand closer to it so that they could hole-in-one all the time. This would seem to be the logical answer to their quest, but that sort of rational thinking has not so far been able to come up with such a straightforward solution to angling's perennial problems.

Mind you, a man who came pretty close to putting fish catching in that 'hole-in-one' situation was the minder of a sluice on a river up which a little-known and unfished-for run of sea-trout took place every spring. He suspended a spinner or two on lines from the bridge over the weir and let them 'fish' all by themselves, simply inspecting his tackle every morning.

While it did produce fish up to 6lb, it was not exactly sporting and was highly illegal as well as short-circuiting several of the concepts which have made angling a method apart.

In spite of the intensity with which persuading a fish to take a hook has been studied, however, we are still seen as a foil for humour. Every hackneyed cartoonist still resorts to the image of that look of amazement as the man holding the rod finds a boot where the fish ought to be.

Be honest, have those of you who, like me, have spent years rather than hours by the water, ever actually seen a boot landed? All sorts of other objects, maybe, but there just cannot be enough people around throwing unwanted footwear into rivers for many of us to perform the most often depicted feat for which we are famous.

I have landed a bike wheel and a mattress in my time as well as hooking but failing to net a bedstead. But never a boot!

There was an occasion when spinning near a bridge I hooked a sack that contained a brick and the long-forgotten remains of what had once been somebody's cat. This was a discovery I made suddenly as the hessian parted while I was trying to disentangle the hook. I suppose anybody who was not near enough to enjoy the aroma might have thought that was funny as well.

There are those among us who do deserve a certain amount of scorn and could be said to bring into question the sanity of all of us. Like the man I heard of who was told by a friend of a particularly good stretch of canal. On an early morning sortie in thick fog, he followed the instructions implicitly, but for the fact that he stopped at the first bridge along the farm track instead of the second.

With the murky dawn what it was, he decided to fish from the parapet itself and got his fishing gear nicely organised before he was startled by an express hurtling beneath him on the down line from Euston.

Fog has led others into trouble as well. There was cause for concern on one of our bigger reservoirs when a boat failed to return on an evening when visibility was akin to that inside the proverbial tram driver's gauntlet. A lot of calling with a loud hailer by bailiffs who knew the water well brought that situation to a happy conclusion.

A pair of well-known fly fishermen did not get away so lightly on another misty evening. Late ashore, they were in a hurry to get away but became so disorientated by the time they had circled their way out of the lodge car park that they headed down a disused road and into the reservoir. They got away with a soaking but it did neither them nor the car any good.

Of course, wettings and fallings-in are all an accepted risk by those who are beside water for long periods. The Law of Averages says somebody just has to get a ducking now and then.

I saw one friend execute a very graceful entry while fixing his keepnet. He leaned a little too far forward while pushing in the bankstick. He thought it was going into hard gravel but it turned out to be soft mud and he somersaulted most spectacularly. The casual observer would probably have wondered what he had done it for.

A lad I was at school with could not swim when he fell in during an angling outing with his family. He discovered a hitherto unknown talent for survival, however, and climbed out on the far bank after swimming across the river. With no bridge for miles in either direction, he simply eased himself back into the water and swam back again.

Not all soakings are the angler's fault either. Like Uncle Charlie's entry into the Old Bedford. He had been fishing comfortably for several hours when a whole section of bank suddenly gave way and slid into the river – with him still sitting on it with a startled look on his face, his rod in his hand and everything from the waist down underwater.

Spectators are not immune from the potential of angling disaster either. Like the man watching the fly casting at the Game Fair at Tatton Park in Cheshire. He had his glasses plucked from his head and flung out into the mere when the back-cast put the hook of the fly neatly round the frame without touching him. The loss of the expensive optics was a real concern, so at the end of the day a lad swam out knowing that as soon as the bottom ooze was stirred up, he would have no chance of finding them.

Following the caster's instructions carefully, however, he duck-dived over the selected spot – and came up with the specs.

Not so lucky was the passer-by who stopped to watch an angler on the Ouse at Ely. Fish were coming steadily and a little group had assembled to look on. The newcomer was just that bit too far to the right when he joined them – and got a size 14 complete with two maggots right in the end of his nose.

He admitted afterwards that it made his eyes water. And so did the injection and removal afterwards. Like sea hooks, which are most often embedded in fishermen's fingers, the barb effectively stopped it being withdrawn; it had to go right in and out the other side!

Perhaps such incidents, however readily appreciated by the onlooker, are not totally humorous; certainly they are not for the principals concerned. But the sort of thing not understood by the outsider and which could appear rather odd is the man scraping gently at the soil under a hawthorn bush and then sieving and sacking it to take away.

If they ask, he will probably mutter something to the effect that it has to do with Black Magic, which won't make them feel any more happily disposed towards him. In truth he would be collecting an ingredient for groundbait. For that beautiful, light, jet-black, peaty earth which accumulates under hedgerows can be used to deadly purpose. Originally used to hold casters for more accurate introduction to the water, there are times when it has other uses.

For instance, the white patch on the riverbed that ordinary white breadcrumbs can produce, is not always liked by the fish. After all, in clear water conditions they will stand out against it and all the time spent over thousands of years by their kind to acquire an effective camouflage is wasted. The black earth helps there.

It also assists by clouding the water, too, making it an area the fish seem to want to investigate. Coloured water means something is disturbing the bottom and it could well be another fish who has found some item of food worth rootling for.

It also makes the bait break up differently. The light brown clay anglers can also be seen scratching around molehills for on other peculiar and little-understood expeditions, is useful for changing the consistency of groundbait, too. If the fisherman knows his craft, he can put in three balls of bait that will break up at differing intervals. The black one will disintegrate first, then the purely crumb one, followed by the brown one with the clay in it. This releases the maggots, casters, worms or whatever over a period so the swim does not have to be disturbed as many times as it would if only the one sort were being thrown in regularly. And, in this context, ground rice is a must for the serious addict. It absorbs water very fast, swells and breaks up a solid ball of bait better than anything.

So, those antics under the hedge that look so peculiar and could give a wrong impression to the benighted, are all part of a much wider and more complex scheme of angling intent.

For the angler is a great innovator and improvisor. The first swingtip was reputedly made from a comb and early swim-feeders were in fact first made to be hair-curlers.

Take, for instance, the talks I used to give periodically when living at Cromer, on how their local newspapers were produced. There was always interest in seeing the hefty lump of lead with the top of the front page in reverse on it that had been used to print one of the titles on the Norwich presses.

That demonstration item did not often go back. It was destined for the pot. Broken down and melted in that old saucepan, it would be poured into the plaster of Paris moulds I made, to reappear as sea leads. Of course, you could always buy weights, but that would not have been anything like as much fun or given half the satisfaction . . . the sort of 'bonus' the angler can understand.

Of course, making use of everyday objects for angling purposes does not need to be as involved as all that, although many thousands derive great pleasure from making floats, tying flies and fiddling with rods. Simply removing the top from a washing-up liquid bottle for use as a bite detector will do. By opening the top and fastening it over the line between butt ring and reel, a very acceptable 'bobbin' indicator is provided. One enterprising tackle firm even made a night indicator for sale by sticking a Betalite into the thing.

Even that is the type of adaptation which the non-participant might find vaguely eccentric.

The sort of activity that can really make them aware of our presence, however, was the action of a sea fisherman I know who pulled up his boat's anchor to find what looked suspiciously like a mine attached to it.

His first reaction was to withdraw as far away from it as he could. But, as his colleague admitted afterwards, being the other end of a 16-foot boat from something designed to blow up a destroyer was not likely to do him much good.

He had heard, too, that some of these things were made to be detonated by changing pressure, so rather than lower it again, he brought it ashore – very carefully – and dumped it alongside the pier.

Not only the pier, but the whole of the sea-front had to be cleared on instructions from the Army bomb disposal team who were called in. They refused to touch it but sent for the Navy experts, who arrived five hours later.

It was, they found, the 'clever' end of a two-part mine laid during the war. One end held enough explosive to wreck a ship, but this was not it. The bit on the beach contained the counting mechanism that would have been set to allow several ships to pass before blowing up one of the more important vessels in the middle of the convoy. Over the intervening years, the two parts had become separated and the harmless drum of rusted metal was all that had caused the panic.

Perhaps it was not what they had intended catching, but it was certainly a bit out of that old boot category!

18

Tackle – the Market
and the Men

FEW industries can be as well blessed with individuals who really care about the things they make and sell as that which supplies the angler. In many cases it is because they use the end products themselves and are passionately involved with the sport.

That is true, not only of the consultants whose names appear on rod handles because they are top anglers, but of the majority of retailers, the salesmen and the heads of some of the major companies. In many cases, it is that love of fishing itself which has led them into the business in which they now earn their livings.

One of the dreams common to most fishermen – along with seeing their name in the record books – is to run their own tackle shop, and there is a constant procession of such newcomers, as well as the more than competent performers with a rod who are already on the other side of the counter. Many an angler, finding he has enough money to fulfil his ambition through Auntie Emily's will or – more likely in recent years – redundancy pay, looks for suitable premises, contacts a few suppliers he knows of because he uses their gear himself, arranges his shelves and stands behind the counter waiting for the rush.

Then he finds it isn't that easy. He may have on display just what he himself would want, but his potential customers do not necessarily agree. And even if he has got the stock right, they want his prices to beat the lowest in the mail order adverts. So he is caught between not selling enough at the proper price to enable him to run the business or shifting it and not making enough profit to carry on. The dream can become a nightmare very quickly and, in something like eighteen months or two years, his money disappears and he goes out of the trade with it.

It is a sad little tale but one that is repeated very regularly. One leading distributor reckons that at any one time there are over 1,000 dealers who either have not been in the trade more than eighteen months or won't be here that far ahead. It's a sobering thought, but it is still such a generally friendly trade to be in if you speak the anglers' language that people won't be put off.

Perhaps it is the very problems of carrying on that make so many of those involved in supplying the angler such good company; they have to be dedicated to have come into it in the first place and totally devoted to stick it. Whatever the reason, I count myself lucky to have worked so closely with them for a decade.

Of course there are exceptions, like the ones who were after my blood when it was disclosed that their rod blanks were being used by somebody else and no one was supposed to know; and the author who reported me to the Press Council when I said the knots described in his book were not the best. But we won't go into that!

The trade is of much more use to the sport than just selling tackle though, a classic example being the recent problem involving swans and lead. It was those in the manufacturing and distributing companies who spear-headed the work that has allowed coarse fishing to continue largely unaffected. They saw the danger first, reacted without pretending the problem was not there and found the answers.

And it cost them money without any prospect of recovering any of it, because most of them are not into lead at all. The list is so long that they can't all be named and I hope those who worked so hard to find substitutes who ought to be on an angling role of fame will forgive me. As well as the associations representing anglers directly, hours are put in by men whose efforts benefit everyone, not just their own firms.

There are a lot of gentlemen in the trade out there to whom

the angler should take off his hat, for they are finding the money he won't stump up himself and then leading his battles from the front. The average fisherman doesn't know they're there let alone appreciate how fortunate he is to have such people on his side.

Their problems don't end there though. They have to plan years in front to have the tackle we are going to want, which means not only very expensive development work but the ever-present chance of rejection at the end of the day. For example, wonderful, latest-technology superb glass rods were still coming through when we all decided we couldn't fish unless the rod said 'Carbon' on the handle.

Since then everybody has been boron balmy before going Kevlar crackers. Who would want to plan a couple of years ahead in that market? They do it.

When a major company outside the trade looked closely at fishing a few years ago, one of the things that staggered them was the virtual lack of brand loyalty. In other markets they understood, customers tend to stay with the products of a company who has satisfied them and whom they have come to trust. But they found that it was possible to draw many anglers away from a brand they had used happily for years simply by going in for the sort of powerful advertising anglers were not used to and making sure the price was right.

The fact that it is now very much a world-wide industry doesn't make supplying the British fisherman any easier either. Part of the trouble is that what a coarse fisherman here means by the very word 'angling' is something different from what the American bass-basher understands from it; the Italian pole man has a picture in his mind far removed from that conjured up by the word for a north-west beachcaster.

So with huge markets, like North America, being catered for, it is obvious that if something made 2 million at a time for them has an application here, the relative few we want are going to be available cheaper than if somebody has to make a few specialist items purely to sell here. This puts our home market manufacturer at a distinct disadvantage unless he can sell some of the things he is asked to make for us overseas. And with angling meaning so many different things that is extremely difficult to do.

The way in which things are affected by what happens in other industries across the globe is shown by the way a tackle firm here was closed as a result of a decision to change the frequency of citizen band radios in the States. Edgar Sealey, who were one of our top rod makers, joined Ken Morritt's Cornish reel company to form Intrepid-Sealey which was in turn taken over by the Gladding Corporation of the States. They were also very much into the CB field and when the waveband was switched by Washington they were left with a load of sets which could not be altered.

An assortment of finance companies and banks who had been backing them stepped in and, when the dust stirred up in Wall Street settled, the Intrepid-Sealey-Gladding operation went down with it. 'Breaker, breaker!' indeed.

No wonder the trade is full of characters. If they were not strong in spirit they would have been broken men and run off screaming to sell biscuits or ladies' tights years ago.

Trade shows and meetings are an eye-opener to those new to the tackle scene. People the angler imagines would be at each others' throats from their adverts, enjoy a chat and a drink together. They examine each others' wares and talk about them, not always disparagingly either.

When somebody drops a real clanger though there is a genuine feeling of concern from most sides. It is an 'Ask not for whom the bell tolls . . .' type of effect.

It is all too easy to come unstuck as well, for the trade is permanently being offered the latest wonder gadget that will revolutionise some facet of the sport. The Americans can't understand why we don't jump at all these things like they do, for over there most of their sales are of 'New' items. We're much more restrained and likely to make things take time to work their way through. Even carbon had been around a while before it became the only material we were interested in.

Perhaps in our market it is because so many of the inventions presented to the trade are bite indicators of one sort or another that you can feel the moans and groans every time someone says he has come up with one. When you realise that one inventor who seems to know what he is doing has patented about twenty of them which nobody wants to put money into to produce commercially, you will see what a difficult market it is.

Years ago I nearly broke a thumb testing an automatic striker-cum-indicator. It fitted on the rod handle and was cocked by pulling on some catapult elastic which was held by a pin. When you got a bite this pin was pulled out, releasing the striking lever. The trouble was it did not just pull the line back; this hefty arm slammed over with enough force to take your thumbnail off. Even if you were quick enough to get your hand out of the firing line, it crunched the cork handle and I reckoned that about three bites would be enough to result in a completely pulped butt on most rods. Not a good idea.

Another device still talked about in the trade was the Mabby. This was a little plastic boat that held about a pint of maggots. They crawled gently out of the container up a ramp so that you could keep a steady bait trail going – once you had towed the craft into position. This was done by throwing a weight upstream of your swim and winching the Mabby into place by pulling on a length of line passing through the weight. There was also an extension arm like a flimsy jib which could be cast over to make it into a bite indicator.

The inventors spent several thousand pounds making and marketing it but no one has ever used one so far as I can discover. An obstacle, of course, was that it infringed the match rules so it could not be used in competitions in any case.

Probably helping the Mabbys to fill a warehouse somewhere are the left over Castamags. The Castamag was a good idea, basically being two containers which screwed together with a sieve in between. Pop maggots and casters in one end, leave it standing a minute and you had them separated. It worked, too, but nobody seemed to want to buy it. They have been a standing joke in the tackle world ever since.

Some really good gadgets – bite detectors among them – have appeared over the years and been largely ignored because the price which can be charged does not allow any advertising to be done to tell people about them. Others have been quite horrible and never had a chance of catching on. Some never got off the drawing board, like one hilarious masterpiece which allowed the angler to fish with a float in a bucket when he was forced to leger. Apart from any other drawback you had to cart a specially adapted bucket about all the time. Another which was actually made had so many bleepers, flashing lights in various colours, swinging arms and Beta-lights it took a quarter of an hour to set it all up every time you struck. It was obviously intended for use in swims where there was little likelihood of there being any fish.

Many splendid products do come on the market though. Towering talents like the late Dick Walker create items that put everyone who fishes in debt to them. His Mark IV set the pace for all future carp rod development – what coarse man does not use the Arlesey bombs – and fly men all know of patterns like the Polystickle, Sweeny Todd and Mrs Palmer as well as his fly rods which Hardys make.

Peter Drennan is another innovator whom anglers have come to regard highly. His Feederlink legers, square bait boxes and see-through floats that don't scare fish in clear water are among tackle now accepted as part of the scene.

There are a host of consultants helping to produce just what our anglers want in conjunction with several companies. And people within the trade who are noted in the fly tying area include Geoffrey Bucknall, Bob Church, John Goddard, Gordon Griffiths, John Veniard and Sue Burgess.

We also have some great rod designers in our midst. People like Tony Fordham, who was the first man to put a spigot ferrule in a rod – and just look and see how your own rod's joints fit together now. Tony has a lovely way of describing the action of rods he doesn't particularly like; he calls them 'Rhubarbish', sometimes adding 'and well stewed at that!'

Jim Bruce, whose work on his firm's Hexagraph rods ends all the inherent weaknesses associated with tubes, is another man who, with partner Ken Walker, has kept British rodmaking among the best in the world, while other fine rods are being made by Daimaru of Japan to the specifications of Omri

Thomas of Normark whose knowledge stems from the days when he was a fly tier.

Then, of course, Daiwa have grown to a position where their Scottish factory can boast of being the biggest rodmaking plant in Europe. It did not happen without a huge investment though. For instance, when they were developing their British rod programme the air freight bills alone were frightening. To make tubular rods you have to have a mandrel, the inner core on which the glass or carbon cloth is rolled before being baked in an oven. These stainless steel rods have to be produced to such fine tolerances that no one in the UK could undertake the work. Most were made to our rod firms' requirements in the USA, but Daiwa's came from their headquarters plant in Japan. When the Ivan Marks Harriers were being prepared, rods were made and tested and then the mandrels returned for alterations many times. Before a single rod was sold, the carriage costs on those rods alone came to more than £3,000.

An interesting offer that helped their sales was that anyone could approach Ivan Marks or fellow consultant Roy Marlow and swop his new gear for the staff man's similar item, just to prove that they were using off-the-shelf tackle just like everybody else.

You can judge what a delightful as well as astute man their former Japanese chief executive Harry Yamomoto is from an incident when he saw me having communication problems with a Scandinavian at a trade show. He came over and commented, 'Some of these foreigners don't speak our language so well, do they?'

If you ever wonder why the price of some specialist gear, like the long carbon poles, seems so high, just remember the true tale of a French manufacturer who was doing very well with the shorter glass poles on the continental market. He felt he had to move into carbon and when I tried an experimental model in which he was attempting to use a mixture of glass and carbon sections, his bill was already more than £12,000 (not francs).

The idea to use glass in the butt and carbon further out where weight was more critical and where, of course, less of the high-priced carbon would be needed, seemed sensible. But he still could not get it right. It sagged here and there and was much too thick to be held comfortably. He made several more prototypes after that before deciding to leave the carbon market to others. As it was, the money was written off but had he succeeded, those massive research costs would have had to be reflected in the final price.

When it is realised that Bruce & Walker, for instance, spent more than £100,000 before we heard of their Hexagraph rods, it is no wonder that equipment using expensive material at the forefront of technological development looks like a luxury for many fishermen.

Tooling up for a reel can be just as costly an exercise. I was shown the drawings for what has become the only all-British fixed-spool reel at least four years before Shakespeare's 2020 came on the market. The trials and tribulations and huge development costs involved in making that closed-face match model were such that it is unlikely anyone else is going to add a second. Which is a shame, because such enterprise and effort on behalf of the UK angler deserves a better reward.

Other people to whom we owe a debt include Barrie Welham, for we have him largely to thank for saving British Fly Reels. And there are few around who have cast a fly line who have not made use of a Gearfly, Rimfly or Dragonfly at some time or another. He is a good angler, too. At the opening day on Rutland Water he found a shoal of rainbows in the morning and, if memory serves me right, had put back eleven by lunchtime. In the afternoon, however, he was fishless and was heard to comment, 'This place isn't what it was you know!'

And that fickleness on behalf of the fish sums up why providing us with tackle and bait is such a chancy, thankless task. Fancy being in a business where, if the catches don't come up to scratch or the river freezes over, nobody buys anything, however good it is!

19

Poles Apart

IT'S intriguing just what the word 'angling' itself means to people in different parts of the world, even in various parts of the UK come to that. Everyone knows the dictionary definition – 'to fish with rod and line' – but there's much more to it than that.

It was probably round about the time of World War I that the British coarse angler stopped taking his catch home to eat as his saltwater and game fishing counterparts still do, very largely. The growth of match fishing, however, allied to the ability to travel more easily to venues further afield, almost certainly had a lot to do with it. Not only was it more difficult to get the fish home in palatable condition but improved living standards played their part in removing the necessity.

Increased pressure on water space also led to an awareness of the need for conservation, anglers quietly leading the way before the sabre-rattlers of the present-day were ever thought of. Though the rod licences still give coarse anglers the right to take a number of fish home if they are above a certain length, not many exercise the privilege.

Those rod licence measurements led to a big area of misunderstanding between anglers in different parts of this country, a disagreement which has only very recently been resolved. That was due to the London angling fraternity sticking to the size limits – not for taking home purposes, but for 'keeping' in a net during a match.

If the fish was not a 'goer' it could not be retained. Undersize fish in the net meant the disqualification of the angler. The move did not altogether have the desired effect for those slightly-too-small fish were treated with a certain amount of contempt, especially those which could not quite be 'stretched' to meet the mark. Worst of all, it led to the alienation of many southern matchmen as far as the rest of the coarse population was concerned. Thank heaven that has been cleared up now.

On the continent, of course, what we regard as the old-fashioned approach that our grandfathers grew out of, still apertains. The fish are usually killed – all of them, however small. This stems partly from their different way of fishing matches. On the other side of the Channel, they fish for a much shorter length of time – due at least in part to their total reliance on the pole which is not as easy to fish well for the five-hour duration of our contests as the more conventional English style is. They also award points for the number of fish caught with extra points for the weight. The upshot is, of course, that someone with lots of small fish is going to beat the one big 'un that weighs roughly the same. The shorter match time also cuts down on the 'lucky dip' aspect, the chance of enticing the one specimen that would settle the issue over here being less. So they set their sights on a different quarry.

With the use of keepnets in the world championships being pioneered by England, however, there are signs that the benefits of conservation are beginning to be realised by some of our continental cousins.

In the USA, where coarse fishing as we know it is in its infancy, there are also signs of Catch and Release programmes gaining in popularity though the main reason for most anglers enjoying the sport is still given as 'Catching something for the pan'. Some of their large tackle concerns are backing events where the fish are all put back, however.

It is perhaps odd that there seems to be a bigger movement towards putting trout back alive on the other side of the Atlantic, all fish being put back even on what we would regard as wild and relatively inaccessible waters in the Rockies.

Perhaps the 'feel' of what fishing is all about in these three parts of the world can best be explained by the story of three boys who each caught an identical fish in their own waters. It is not so much the catching of the fish but the reaction to what happened to it that underlines the fact that we are still poles apart (if you'll pardon the pun).

Case number one is a 12-year-old English lad who is following in his father's footsteps and has been allowed to go off on a carp fishing expedition with a couple of friends during the school holidays. He comes home and bursts in clutching a carp of around 4lb.

'Look at this!' he shouts. But Johnny's joy is short-lived, for when the would-be Walton sees the look on Dad's face he knows the pleasure in his achievement is not shared . . . he has committed a sin. Instead of praise, he finds himself in disgrace for having killed the fish. He is given a lecture on the need for conservation and it is explained to him in no uncertain terms that the place for that carp was back in the lake, not in the house.

The reason is partly to do with the fact that his father knows the fish was one he and his fellow club members had bought and put in the lake as a 4-inch stock fish four winters before to improve the sport in the local water.

Young Pierre's story is much the same in that he and a few of his friends have been down to the local canal where the French lad has been fortunate to contact one of the carp that live among the smaller fish they were really seeking. Having landed it on his pole tackle, however, there was no question of what to do with it. They had no keepnet, so he killed it right away instead of leaving it in a net in the water until it was time to come home as the British boy did.

Now, Pierre carries his trophy home with pride and is greeted with a good deal of warmth by his family. His father shows it to his fishing neighbours as proof of the boy's ability while his mother immediately begins to plan the best way of cooking it, for she will make it into a fine meal. He would have been thought of as a bit odd if he had even mentioned to his pals that he might put it back once he had landed it.

Elmer, too, would not have intended catching a carp in the first place. Not because he was after smaller stuff and did not think he could have landed one; he would not have thought about carp at all. In the USA they have a rating little higher than vermin and if he got his hook into one by mistake he would have shaken it off rather than waste time landing it as likely as not. Having caught one, however, he dumped it unceremoniously up the bank amid taunting laughter from his fishing mates.

I was told of a man fishing the Great Lakes for pike who played a big fish for some time before realising it was a carp he had on. Though it was a fish well on the way to 50lb, once he knew what it was that had taken his spinner, he cut his line to the amazement of the British angler who was with him. That's how they regard them over there. When they hear that we actually have people in England who buy carp with which to stock waters, they must think we're crazy. And the continental angler would agree with them once he knew we did not propose to eat them.

I don't think it is a question of who is right and who is ignorant. It is a matter of custom having grown out of the needs created by the differing backgrounds of the anglers themselves. We do tend to believe that the French and other continentals are barbaric for taking home all the fish they catch. They feel we are stupid to insist on keeping fish alive in nets and then putting them back. In truth, when the results of matches in some of our waters are examined, it makes me wonder just what we have got to show for fifty years of trying to conserve our fish by returning them.

Almost certainly, the American fish stocks – except the sport species – have not been guarded as closely as our own. The reason is that the resource has so much more recently been tapped that any inroads into the stock is not readily discernible in many areas, allied to the few anglers who are interested in the type of fishing which our coarse men think of as the ultimate in angling competence.

The widening of knowledge by travelling anglers and the interchange of ideas through competitions and publications is, however, making many examine afresh their own outlook. You only have to think of pole fishing to understand the results of this in the UK. Not long since, it was treated as a peculiarly Home Counties sort of activity that was all right on the Thames and thereabouts but not far beyond.

That was in its clumsy, heavy cane form. Then the

matchmen of the north and the Midlands strangely enough, cottoned on to what the continentals had to teach us and took British angling into a whole new area. Now the southern anglers are hot on the pole trail as well.

The educational process has also worked in the reverse direction, with Frenchmen talking of fishing *à l'Anglaise*. But it does not seem to have the same impetus – not yet anyway. With trout fishing, too, they are beginning to realise what a lot we have to teach them. The French fly fisherman is still in the short-rod, brook and dry fly era that pervaded our game fishing scene in the thirties. Only very recently have they become aware of the sport to be had from stillwaters with heavier lines, bigger lures and stiffer, longer rods.

The American fly fisherman is in very much the same state. Over there an 8-foot rod is considered a long one whereas most fly fishermen in the UK don't even possess a rod under 9 feet.

But if float fishing and fly fishing are areas where there is a sign of some advance in understanding, legering is a different proposition altogether for that is an example of a type of fishing which is very largely peculiar to ourselves. Perhaps the fact that world championship rules prevent legering has something to do with it, for they state that all the weight must be supported by the float.

If – or perhaps, when – they allow us to show what we can do with our leger tactics, they are in for a real hammering. I'm sure of that; and I suspect most of them are as well, which could delay the change. It's just something they know nothing about.

I recall trying to explain to a group of Italians on one of the British stands at the big SPOGA exhibition in Cologne some years ago what a swingtip was for. The head of the company showing the device opted out of trying to tell them about it and suckered me into the situation. With negligible Italian and with their English being even worse, the only thing for it was a demonstration.

It was a perfectly ordinary swingtip with a screw-in fitting for the rod's tip ring and flexible link to dangling indicator.

These visitors could not see how it could work. So I borrowed a rod and reel from a nearby firm, rigged up the tip and found a friend to be the fish to give me a bite.

Soon the Italians got the idea and were taking it in turns to register a bite and then let me 'play' them up and down the aisle. Then, of course, they had a go with the rod and played me and each other.

If it was not exactly a show-stopper, it certainly created a fair bit of congestion – and interest. They went off talking in their own passionate way about the whole idea of being able to tell if you had a bite without there being a float in the set-up. It was totally new to them and they could see the application of this form of bite-registration to their own fishing.

Mind you, they didn't actually order any. But the day will come!

20
How to Achieve
a Test Ban

WHENEVER another of those great summit meetings takes place at which the leaders of the super powers face each other across an imposing table in a bid to determine how they are going to refrain from blowing us all to pieces for a few more years, I always feel they are in the wrong place and trying to come to terms in less than perfect circumstances.

All those advisers, security men and political planners should be banished while the main protagonists are taken to a chalk stream in its peaceful valley, kitted out with a rod apiece and left to talk out their differences while they try to sort out the much more pressing need – how they can each catch trout.

There would have to be an interpreter, of course, but he would be their angling guide, their ghillie, only able to offer advice on the fishing. Lots of men of distinction in their own fields find fulfilment of another kind in the contemplation that is part of the pleasure from days in such surroundings – they recharge their batteries, replenish their spirits and restore their souls there. One of these who speaks Russian and English would be just the person to provide the link . . . his angling knowledge being the Missing Link at all those hope-dashing, high-powered assemblies.

Passing through him, any bitterness would be filtered from the dialogue; no one with a vested interest in arms sales would be able to intervene. Getting them back to their roots, reducing their convoluted thinking down to that basic desire to catch a wary fish would join them in a common purpose which might just make them realise they are not really all that impossibly separated and always on opposite sides at all.

If my dream could be taken a stage further and they were to meet on the bank regularly as joint custodians of the stream, angling could really make the world a safer place. For no one responsible for stocking a river for posterity could possibly push that button, could they!

The world would be a better place, too, if all we more humble mortals had a day now and then on such a river, not necessarily always sharing the occasion with those we view as most pleasant and companionable. Of course, the company does help make such occasions truly magic interludes in life, but a lot of misunderstandings could be resolved in that environment – even if our catches were not always note-worthy.

Perhaps the fortunate ones who habitually find themselves in these favoured surroundings do not fully comprehend what effect these infrequent incursions into their domain can have on a basically 'coarse' fellow. It isn't simply the different fishing, but a change in the attitude to life that is discernible.

To illustrate just what I mean, the best thing I can do is let you into the secrets of one such day.

The man I had to see on business rented a rod on one of the best stretches of the River Test, that Mecca of fly fishermen the world over, the water where it all began.

'We can talk as well there as in my office,' he said. No objection was raised.

An early start saw me at his home on time and the pair of us were in rural Hampshire by mid-morning, just in time to be greeted by a torrential downpour as the threatening clouds decided this was the time and place to empty themselves.

The little thatched fishing hut ½ mile along the bank pro-vided a much-needed civilised touch in the conditions. With the incentive to hurry our preparations removed, time was spent discussing our beat for the day, the fish it held, where they were likely to be found, the best approach . . .

By the time the rain eased – I could not quite contain myself until it stopped completely – I had an idea of the geography of the water. There was the long straight of the Test itself, shallow on one bank, deeper on the other; the hole under the support of the footbridge near the hut; the spate through the runnel down to the broad corner where it met the feeder stream 100 yards through the reeds and willows; the meeting with the main stream again below the weir.

And there were the seats – planks nailed to tree trunks – that fitted perfectly into the surroundings of the trimmed bankside grass with its fringe of reed left for concealment. Seats where statesmen, men of empire, even, had sat – perhaps even Skues himself.

The rules were upstream dry fly and nymph only and to help the atmosphere, I abandoned the boron and carbon of the reservoir for a split-cane rod. With no long casting called for the sweet action of the natural material could add to the enjoyment as well as the mood.

Soon a rainbow trout around the pound and a half mark accepted a Pheasant Tail and it was a refreshing change for a Fenman to actually see the take beneath the surface of the crystal water.

It had seemed odd in some ways that with all the money being paid for the right to fish here – immense by coarse standards – that the limit imposed was a mere three fish (pardon, a brace and a half!) But now it began to add up. With one on the bank, the pressure which most fishermen place on themselves was removed.

The vast majority of trout men and all coarse anglers assume this burden when they pick up their rod, being out for a tally of eight fish – or whatever the stipulated target might be – or after as many fish as we can collect to put on the scales.

Now there was time to saunter, to dawdle, to observe. The need to rush was no longer present; far better to make the Polaroids do their work, to search out a better fish. After all, we could catch only two more fish all day!

With a wind freshening after the chilling rain, it was not a good day. We did not have the advantage of a hatch of flies to induce a feeding frenzy among the fish. My mentor knew there were many more in the water before us than we were going to see a trace of, but it was still inspiring to be able to run the fly through the likely holding areas.

144

Where the water tumbled down a narrow gravel chute from river to backwater, a deep scour was inhabited by a wily rainbow of at least 6lb. By inching round a stout willow, it could be seen lazily rising every now and then to inspect potential meals being served for him by the current.

'I thought he might have been caught by now,' my friend said. 'Everybody knows he's there but he hasn't got that size by being stupid.' And, sportsman that he is, he refused to try for him but gave me the honour. Perhaps he remembered too well previous attempts.

The big rainbow took a half-hearted peep at a couple of flies when I did manage to waggle them into place under the overhanging, weeping branches which provided an aerial roof to his domain. I finally did what I suspected many others had done before me, I scared him sufficiently for him not to budge from the bottom of his lie. I retired hurt.

My companion did try later, but with the same result. I imagine that crafty old trout eventually succumbed to old age, for anyone hooking him there had precious little hope of landing him. Still, it would have been great to have had the chance to see if I could have achieved it.

Another holt where I was put on to a fish was among the tree roots of the undercut bank as that side stream poured into the feeder below, forming a wide and gravel-headed pool. A brown trout was sheltering from the spate, gliding out to sip in the odd delicacy. The only way to tempt him was to flick a fly on a short line from the rod end, for trees overhead precluded any semblance of a proper cast.

From where even this awkward movement was possible, however, he could not be seen and, as any 'take' was liable to be ejected very quickly or the fish buried in the tangled protection he had sought out, the man who was spending his day in pursuit of my enjoyment stationed himself upstream as an observer. From there, he could see what was happening and he talked me into catching it.

'That's a bit too far out. It wants to land just upstream of that blade of grass sticking out of the bank. No more than a foot out.'

'Hold it! He's come to look at it. He's let it go.'

'Do the same thing again.'

'No, he's interested, but he won't come up far for it. Cast a couple of feet further up so it can sink deeper by the time he sees it.'

Wiggle-waggle. Wiggle-waggle. Sideways back and forth passed the end of the rod. Plop! Wait . . .

'He's taken it. Strike!' And, as the water erupted and the line whizzed across the stream, he added, 'You've got him!'

It wasn't a monster, but that 2½lb Test brownie was perfect. Glowingly yellow, with the pure gold enhanced by the darkly patterned spots, my instincts were all for putting him back. It was not the thing to do though and when we dined on him I must confess to being glad we hadn't.

The third fish that would have added the half to the brace, did not show before we had to leave without any insect life daring to hatch into the biting evening. It did not matter.

Two fish between two of us – for the man who offered the invitation had not really done much more than make sure I had the ones that were caught – may not have amounted to much of a bag. But the day was memorable.

We had talked of many things besides trout and by the time I left on the long, dark drive north, we knew much about each other. His business plans, which I had gone to discuss and were the excuse that had taken me there, were much clearer than any office briefing could have made them.

Perhaps more importantly, we had touched on much more personal, nearer-the-heart things. He had even told me of the daughter dying in a car crash not many months before – a privileged, personal insight into a corner of his secret self that left a mark no less enduring than the picture of that treasured trout etched indelibly in my mind.

If the honest unburdening of real trouble can be invoked by an unhurried day in pursuit of a few fish I know that differences over mere political issues that cannot possibly be more deeply felt, would benefit from an airing in similar circumstances. Never mind Geneva and the United Nations. Let's get 'em on the Test!

21
The Killjoys

I WOULDN'T leave your car there,' he said. 'It could get covered with spots that'll take the paint off.'

I had parked my car off the road and, as I thought, out of harm's way before setting off with my tackle down the bank. The warning from the friendly farmer advised me otherwise however.

'I'm going to spray these 'taters and the stuff's a bit corrosive,' he explained.

'What on earth are you using that takes paint off cars?' I asked him.

'Oh, it's some new potent stuff out this year. I wanted what I've used the past couple of years but they've withdrawn it from the market. They're always doing that. You find something that does the job a treat, then they find a problem with something it does on the side that isn't very pleasant and they stop making it and you have to try something else.'

So I moved the car well upwind. All the time I was fishing I kept wondering about two things:

What would this 'new stuff' that would take paint off cars do to the luckless people who would end up eating those potatoes?

And what effect would it have when it got into the river? For end up in the river it certainly would, just like all the drifting spray dumped on the land from aircraft that taints the air every year giving those living nearby sore throats.

I'm not the only angler who has had to put his brolly up to guard against the drift from ill-aimed sorties that obviously douse the rivers direct with chemicals that can cause unknown and untold havoc to all forms of wildlife.

It might seem odd to talk about pollution in a book about

fishing for fun but there are killjoys around other than the easily-spotted antis. There won't be much enjoyment if there are no fish and the fishing has got steadily worse in much of the largely arable areas like Eastern England over recent years.

We had the outcry against the zander, of course, and he was made the scapegoat for the demise. But he wasn't responsible for it all. Indeed, had the waters been healthy the zander level would have stabilised along with the pike. They would hardly have been noticed by now.

The real reason for the demise of the 'prey species' – which really includes everything, for pike and zander are not averse to eating pike and zander any more than roach are opposed to eating roach eggs – is much more complicated than that. It is all tied up with new towns, old sewers and massive changes in farming.

Places like Milton Keynes have appeared and all the water that is being used there as well as in double-sized cities like Peterborough and Northampton would have flushed out the rivers not many years ago. Now most of the water coming down is 'second hand.'

There is the next part of the problem. Not only are many sewage works overloaded to the point where they have a job to cope, but much of the water coming out of taps in the first place is not up to the standards laid down by the EEC. This is partly due to the level of chemicals, mainly nitrate fertilisers, that are leaching into many water courses.

With permission given for millions and millions of gallons to be pumped out for irrigation – so much so that a couple of summers ago a large part of the Fen water system flowed *backwards* for weeks – more is being sucked out than is coming in. So any impurity or dangerous substance getting into the rivers is not going to be diluted and washed away. It is going to become concentrated and stay there a long time.

Which brings us back to the farming angle. Did you know that in 1984 more than one thousand million tons of chemicals were used by Britain's farming industry? It is easy simply to blame the farmer, but he is running a business and with pressure on him growing he has to push up the yield as much as he can.

I know one farmer who has stopped using anything he is not sure about since two men died suddenly after spraying his crops. Both died from 'natural causes' but he had enough doubts in his own mind to keep anything like the car-damaging potato spray away from his land. There are, of course, other really caring people around and I don't want to malign them. There is, however, lots of evidence that there are others who ignore the potential dangers of which they are well aware.

Some farmers are real friends of the earth, protecting the environment in a way that only they can. But there are others who would cheerfully kill every living creature if they thought it would bring them an extra few quid an acre. For most, it is not as clear cut as that, it is just that they go on using all those herbicides, insecticides and pesticides along with the fertilisers when the long-term effects can only be guessed at.

What we are sure of is that if no more were to be used, it would be years, if ever, before the residual effect would disappear. And, sooner or later, every drop will end up in a water course. The level of dilution is unlikely to improve; the toxins become concentrated in the stagnating water.

We could be on the threshold of an ecological disaster, the first effects of which are already becoming apparent – at least they are to the angler.

Not long ago, you could lie back in the grass on a hot day and spot the skylark who was chattering his persistent song high overhead. It was something you could do when the fish stopped biting wherever you were. There were swallows, swifts and martins, too, busy chasing insects and dipping for a snatched drop of water as they skimmed the surface. You're lucky to see them now.

They did not disappear suddenly; they just slipped away a few at a time over the years and no longer come to spend the summer with us. I had not realised just how much we missed them until a recent trip to France and Spain. The evenings there were filled with the screeches of insect-hunting birds as they whirled round the towers of the churches wherever we stopped. Clouds of them dived from their muddy nests under the eaves and swept the air clean of gnats and midges.

So this was where they had gone.

The poisons that have worked as far as removing the pests from our farms is concerned have broken the food chain of the rivers, too.

Bloodworm is a conflict-causing coarse fish bait, being banned on more British waters than any other. The argument is that it isn't fair because it is too expensive for everyone to buy and not all anglers can get their own; the average angler cannot afford enough of these little red larvae of the gnat.

Whatever you think about the bans, I wish you well if you try to find some in many parts of the country – the intensively farmed parts. Last time I set about the messy job of drawing a blade fixed to a pole through the bottom mud to 'scrape' some up I could find hardly any in drains that used to be packed with 'em.

The swallows knew they weren't there before then. And if the birds know, so do the fish. How many of them – not just little fish but chunky tench and bream – spent their summers rootling in the silt for these tasty morsels? They are either on a different diet or have left now.

The snails that lived on the lilies have been struck off the menu on many waters as well, simply because the water weeds are not there either.

Increased boating activity has removed much of them – just look at the 'popular' bits of the Broads and other holiday waterways. Then, of course, there are the sprays which are the modern method of saving having to cut the weeds.

In that super summer of '76 one river I know well was 'treated' twice. Every lily was exterminated, poison soaking into the plant through the floating leaves and killing the root. That water will never be the same again, especially as dredging not long after, took the far bank shelf from 3 or 4 feet to 10 or 11 feet.

Somehow fish survive. They are still there to be caught if not in such numbers. But it is a rare occasion when you can keep them feeding for more than an hour or so. If you get them together on your bait, pretty soon any predator around spots them. Instead of melting back into the weed cover and coming out again when he's gone, they are chased away. If they do feed again, it will probably be well away from your offerings.

How we halt the adverse effects threatening our rivers is a matter that exercised the minds of bodies like the Angling Foundation many times over the years during which I had the privilege to serve on their council. Part of the problem is that many anglers are partly to blame, not for causing the damage but for saying nothing about it when they knew it was going on. The politically motivated fishermen who are the ones giving their time to run the clubs have been afraid to rock the boat in many cases.

After all, they rented their waters from the very authorities who were primarily responsible for either causing or failing to prevent much of the damage. Many more relied on farmers for access to waters, even if they didn't rent the fishing from them.

And, all the time, there was this naive hope in many minds that the water authorities were looking after our interests. Wasn't there legislation that said they had to? Weren't we paying rod licence money to them for just that purpose?

The late Dick Walker's astute comment that putting the water industry in charge of pollution control was like staffing Scotland Yard with practising burglars was so profound it should be inscribed above the entrance to the Department of the Environment.

I was told by a man whose job it once was to monitor pollution for one huge area what happened to him. When he prepared a report on a damaging situation he was advised, 'I wouldn't pass it along if I were you.' He did and it came back to him from his immediate superior with the further advice, 'If news of this gets out we'll take a lot of stick and it will cost thousands of pounds to put it right. I don't know where the money will come from but I wouldn't be surprised if staff cuts weren't involved. See what I mean? If I were you I'd just file it away.'

He left them not long afterwards anyway but I wonder how many more are still there, filing their reports away and making sure there aren't even any reports wherever possible.

It's a case not so much of ignorance being bliss but being

cheap. If the public don't know and are encouraged to disregard any warnings we might sound, they don't call for action; this means no one has to find the money to do anything; the rates don't go up; and the ship of state glides smoothly on its way.

When august bodies like the Nature Conservancy Council spend their energies on matters like swans and lead shot it makes you feel they haven't really got their sights properly adjusted. With the swan population growing anyway, their efforts will make no major difference even if they have made anglers clean up their act. It was an emotive issue from which they could emerge in the public eye as victorious champions for a cause.

Perhaps they don't want to get into important battles they feel they can't win. Perhaps they don't even acknowledge the existence of the wider, dramatically more vital issues out there that will sooner or later affect everybody, not just fishermen.

They ought to listen to some of those contemplative men who spend quiet hours trying to catch a few fish. For we are part of the biggest conservation-minded, environmental group in the land – the anglers. It's a pity we are probably also the worst organised.

22

The Doctor Fish

WE can't leave a book that is really about the pleasure to be derived from fishing with the sour strains of politics ringing in our ears, even though it is vital that anyone who is likely to want to go fishing again should know what we are up against.

So let's look to the future with optimism in the shape of the tench.

Old timers in the Fens referred to them as the 'Doctor Fish'. The reason most often given was that small fish who rubbed against them recovered from wounds and parasites. Tench slime was a powerful antiseptic that would not only work on fish but would heal cuts too, they said.

I never found anyone who had actually tried it, of course, but it's such a nice tale I'd like it to be true. The rate at which most of us catch tench, however, we'd be pretty sick before we filled that particular prescription I reckon. Stick to iodine!

One thing is certain, these olive-scaled masters of the disappearing trick are responsible for an immeasurable amount of spirit lifting. If nothing else, they do earn the title of doctors of psychology every summer. They are taken in cold conditions sometimes, I know, but it is summer sport to which they really belong.

Searchers after massive carp probably outnumber tench fishers today, but you need special equipment to tame them. Hook a carp on your roach gear and, unless he is pretty stupid and/or you are very lucky, you really have little chance of seeing a satisfactory end to the encounter.

But the tench is of a size that gives you a possibility of winning – even with a roach pole – as long as you haven't got the frailest of tackle and he isn't unusually large.

With a lazy mist drifting away across the weeded water and dragonflies practising their balancing act on reedstems or showing off their aerobatic prowess, you can feel tench should be around. Tell-tale sheets of minute bubbles often give the game away. They're in the swim making it a time of intense anticipation that causes the angler's blood to tingle.

Though the fish are undoubtedly there and apparently feeding, they are not always caught. I was taken to a lake early one summer morning by a man who knew the water like the proverbial back of his hand. He showed two of us a corner where he told us to expect the tench to arrive on their morning patrol at 7 o'clock.

'Put your bait in under your rod tips,' he said, 'then just wait and see. Try what hookbait you fancy but you won't catch one.'

Nothing moved until just before 7am when we saw those give-away pin-prick bubbles along the bank, just odd disturbances of the surface here and there. The path the fish followed brought them on to our bait at 7, just as we had been told. For three-quarters of an hour or so we tried all manner of baits and tackle without any response though the water in front of us looked as if a kettle were boiling heartily down below the entire time. There was so much activity in the swim, it was a wonder neither of us foulhooked one before they simply moved on and the bubbling stopped.

We had the feeling then that trout anglers know when fish are feeding greedily but ignore any fly with a line attached to it. Frustration is far too mild a word for the feeling.

Our host only laughed, for we were among many who had been subjected to the same treatment by those tench over the years.

They've had the laugh on me several other times, too – two occasions in particular. The first was when Colin Dyson and I fished a Norfolk lake later to become famous for its huge tench. It was an idyllic summer evening and we used our Broads boat tactics, baiting the same swim and fishing from either side of a big hawthorn bush. One of us would cast, then the other would cast further out, drawing his tackle back until the two floats were a foot apart.

I soon had a decent fish but then there was a long wait before Colin caught one, and another, and another . . . By the time he had four or five I had tried everything without having another bite. We compared tackle and I adjusted mine until it was hook for hook, shot for shot exactly the same as his. I even tried his bait.

When we packed up in the dark, he had ten tench in his net. I had just that first one. We've never been able to fathom out why.

A similar performance was put on years later during an early morning session with Peter Bailey of Chatteris. We had dragged the swims on the Forty Foot and baited up the night before. Things were perfect that first morning. By the time I had three tench, I was feeling sorry for Peter who hadn't had a bite a few yards away. Then he had one, and another . . . Oh no, I thought, it's going to happen again.

It did. He ended with twelve—a terrific haul for a Fen drain – while I still had that first three. It obviously doesn't do to hope someone else is going to have one when you're after tench. They might have them all!

If the trout is the racehorse of the piscatorial world, the tench is the shire, humping his shoulders stolidly and pulling in his own direction, not rushing and cavorting, though he can hurry if he has a mind to. Normally, he doesn't dash for freedom; he powers his way towards the weed cover he knows so well and will leave you playing nothing but vegetation if he can make it to his sanctuary.

But if you beat him, that sturdy shape, silk-soft flank and baleful red eye make you know you've achieved something out of the ordinary. There is something about a tench that makes you feel good, even if he is only a little one, for tiny tench are probably the jolliest fish of all.

Yet these handsome creatures can live and thrive in places other species can't abide. With the eel, they share that magic ability to turn up where least expected and can survive against huge odds.

I knew of a trout water that was drained regularly for

cleaning and coarse fish removal along with the fish cropping. Mysteriously, tench always seemed to be there. So, next time, the owner left it empty for a fortnight for the bottom mud to crack in the sun. When he went to open the sluice to refill it, he moved an old plastic sack near the hatch. In the thick ooze beneath it were several tench, packed tightly in the only damp patch left to them – and alive.

He let them stay.

Every coarse angler has stories of tench, landed and lost. They create the sort of situations you remember. I recall one Norfolk fisherman who knew his way round the Broads well enough to have won a lot of matches and who had never caught one. He had a feeling something was wrong with him.

They don't always let you down though, like the most satisfying of all the thousands of fish I've caught.

Out in the vast flatness of the Fens there used to be a tall, brick, pumping station chimney that acted like a beacon when we went on our regular Saturday afternoon expeditions. Its engine sucked water from a network of drains that stretched for miles across the low land. When the machinery was doing its persistent chuffing and coughing it was a waste of time going near. But if you caught it as the water from the land drained into the back channels and restored a reasonable level, bringing colour and food, the fishing was likely to be great.

It didn't coincide with our outings very often, most of the time being too low, or clear, and we ignored it for wider waters. Over the years though, we caught all sorts of fish in the basin at the rear of that pump and got to know the man who ran it. He was always proud to show off the inside of his charge where you 'could eat your dinner' off the floor let alone the brass-bound engine. Somehow we never landed a single tench though we knew they were there.

Many years later I went back. The chimney had gone along with the noisy steam engine. A smart new pump which didn't gobble up great lumps of coal was there. So was a neat bungalow in place of the cottage, with a lawn running down to the basin. The same engineer was still presiding over his piece of the world though, and after a bit of diplomatic harking back to the old days, he let me try again for those elusive tench.

I was there and fishing at first light next day. The first bite produced really solid resistance that had me wondering before I saw that yet again a pike had put in an unwanted appearance and upset my tenchy calculations. It was a good one too, especially for this 3lb line.

Two men working with a tractor in the field opposite were attracted by the hooped rod and stopped to watch as the fish swam gently away only to be guided back by side pressure time and time again. As it went round and round, they set off up the field. Back to the headland again, they paused to see how things were going on. The answer was not too well, especially as the landing net was about a third as wide as the pike was long.

It was on their next visit several minutes later that they cheered the conclusion of the scrap. As the pike made yet another circuit, I eased the net towards it so that the water pressure kept it open. The pike was probably mesmerised by boredom by now for it followed the same route and swam straight in. I dropped the rod, grabbed the rim and lifted it clear. It weighed 12½lb.

It was long after things had quietened down and the sun had climbed high before I had another bite. This yielded the first of three tench, none of them more than 2½lb, but it did show I had learned something since I was there before.

That evening I went back with two other fishermen – my father and my son. And just as it was getting dark and we were talking about 'the last cast', I hooked a good fish that was determined to get into weeds right under my feet. It was an unusual and dogged scrap with the rod bent double as I had to keep levering outwards. In the end he tired so that I could inch him to the surface and over the waiting net.

The only scales available stopped at 4lb. He banged them down. With no flashgun either, we decided not to keep him for photographing and proper weighing. We gently returned him to the murky water, not knowing how big he really was and without a picture other than the ones we had in our minds.

It didn't matter a bit. The witnesses were impeccable and I didn't mind if no one believed us even if they ever heard about it.

For that is what fishing is all about; personal satisfaction and the gratification of instincts which helps put the rest of life in a clearer perspective. For once, I had got there on the right day and that made all the times when I had got there a day too late worth while.